An E-mail

Dear Rev. Newman:

I find it astounding you and I should share a seat on a plane and you were able to change my outlook on life. I turned away from my faith due to my son being guilty of murder and I can't believe I shared this dark secret with a total stranger on a flight. Not only did you give me plenty to think about in our conversation but receiving your email with the rough draft of your book gave me plenty of insight to what I needed to do.

Thanks to you and your book for the first time in a long time I could see clearly what I had to do for me and my family without feeling any quilt about my sons' situation. I will continue to love and support him the best I can but your were right in stating I can not change his situation so I have to put my energy into what is best for me, my wife, and our other children. You lifted a dark cloud from over our family and I can see a brighter future for all of us.

From the bottom of my heart "Thank You!" and I hope your book helps others as it has helped me.

    Name withheld by request

    Oklahoma City, Oklahoma

Grief Behind Bars

A Look At Grieving For Families, Inmates,
Professionals, And Those On Death Row

By Dan Newman

Grief Behind Bars

Copyright ©2012 Daniel M. Newman

Forward

At last, here is a book that explains grief without judgment. Dr. Dan Newman writes with compassion and common sense about those aspects of a process few comprehend. To express bereavement in all its facets is something needed in both the professional and personal areas of information. Being involved with Thanatology for so many years, I discovered most people interpret grief as death. Loss is a far larger picture as Dr. Newman describes so well. Loss of freedom, of hope, of relationships – there are so many losses in people's lives. Loss of job, of home, of country, of self worth; the list is endless.

I have been a bereavement specialist since 1974, working both with a patient who was on Death Row and subsequently executed, and am currently on the Advisory Board of the Montgomery County Parents of Murdered Children. Being on both ends of the problem I appreciate Dr. Newman's non judgmental, factual rendering of how grief affects everyone involved. Some years ago, when I had a radio show, a woman called in to say she was the mother of a murdered child. It was heart rending to be sure and as anyone knows who works with bereaved parents; they take a chunk of you each time it happens.

She went on to recount sitting in the courtroom at the trial of the murderer, feeling rage, bitterness, deep, almost untouchable sadness, when she saw the mother of the accused. She then said 'my heart went out to her – she too had lost a son'. Such forgiveness! I know a lot of people would argue the point that at least her son was alive but he was still her child who was to be put to death. Someone once said to me "I suppose you get used to it after all these years". When that happens, I quit. I know Dan feels the same way.

In writing this forward, I am honored to know Dan Newman. I have worked with him, confided in him, and am always amazed at his innate wisdom. In the book he states he has suffered many close losses and tragedies in his life: I personally want to know more of that, how he coped and dealt with shock and extreme pain. Suffice it to say that having been given the privilege of writing this piece, I discovered how impossible it is to be clinically professional in so doing. This subject is volatile and it takes courage to address it. This is a career of the heart, avocation, not a job. Not everyone can do it. Are we special as Thanatologists? Absolutely! There is no place for control of circumstances in these cases. The Serenity Prayer in action: do something you can do something about and let the rest go. Do you know how hard that is when one wants to change was is into what we would like it to be?

My experience with Death Row was somewhat different from Dan's in that the Death Row Prison Staff were some of the most compassionate men I have ever met. Certainly I went through the games of getting there in the first place, but there were no cuffs, no glass, and no telephones between us. Each state has its own methods, and one has to adhere to them. In this book, the reader can see the enormous courage Dan has, to mediate amongst not only the prisoner, but all of the families involved. Even though people do not like to discuss death, it needs to be done. It is easier to put a program of Sex Education in schools these days, than studies of Grief and Loss. Even recovery programs don't know of the issues surrounding Grief.

People cannot recover from loss without dealing with their grief and unfinished business. It is my hope that this excellent book, so personal and honest, will reach schools and universities, particularly those dealing with law enforcement, mental health and counseling degrees. One cannot travel life without understanding grief. This book is a challenge to those who are unilateral in their belief system. It will not reach all people – what book does – but maybe just maybe it will open opportunities for discussion on how to deal with this ever growing challenge.

Dan Newman: Veteran, Interfaith Minister, Spiritual Counselor, Healer, Educator, artist, and now author, is a man of the 21st century. His courage in all aspects of life is coupled with his enormously inviting sense of humor – he is one funny man. Add to that a spirituality of the highest order and we have, as Og Mandino would describe, a Human Becoming. Dan hasn't finished by far. His work is constantly evolving as is he. Reverend Dan Newman PhD, DD is a man of the times and in those times lay more and more challenges to uncover and bring all of our awareness. Thank you Dan, for this uncomplicated and comprehensive, well written book.

    –   Yvonne Kaye. PhD, MSC

Dedication

To Jan Borgman and the members of GriefWork, you gave me the strength and courage to write this book.

To Dr. Yvonne Kaye, a special thank-you for believing in me.

To Steve Elliott, my appreciation for all your computer help.

To Dr. Kirk Prine and Donny Lobree, many blessings for your love & faith.

And to the small group of friends who took time out of their busy lives to read the rough draft and relate their honest opinions and suggestions to create a better book, I offer my prayers and thanks.

Acknowledgments

Thank you to the families and inmates who gave me permission to write about my experiences while working with them through their grief issues. You let me inside your personal lives and shared with me your fears and pain in order that I might better understand your grieving process.

To all the members of GriefWork who gave me support and assisted me by relating all of their experiences working as grief counselors: you challenged me to write this book for the benefit of counselors and clergy who work with grief in the world of the incarcerated and their families.

From the bottom of my heart many thanks go out to Chuck Schramm who let me take on this challenge and gave me support when things got really crazy and I seemed lost.

Thanks to Dr. Kirk Prine and Donald Lobree who gave me the idea and the realization this was something I not only could, but should, write about.

Thanks also to Lynne Klippel's and Christine Kloser's "Love Your Life Publishing, Inc.", for without your expertise and guidance I could not have written this book.

Table of Contents

Introduction

Working With The Incarcerated, Death Row Inmates, And Their Families

If you have experience working with the incarcerated and their families you may or may not have figured out their grieving process. When I started working with my first death row inmate, I realized all of the grieving protocol I had been taught just didn't work that well.

I understood the steps of the grieving process and how they could be attained only to resurface at any given time. This rings true when working with both the victim's family and the family of the perpetrator.

Working as a Senior Health Educator and Interfaith Minister I have been in and out of treatment centers, recovery centers, jails, and prisons for over 20 years. My primary job is to educate inmates on the prevention and reduction of HIV/AIDS, STIs, alcohol and drug abuse, stress management, and how to live a healthy, clean, and sober life.

During this process, I discovered just how much grief and the grieving process interfered with their recovery, how it not only affected the individuals incarcerated but also their families as well.

Even someone who is serving thirty to ninety days for alcohol or drug abuse goes through a grieving process as do their families and loved ones.

When you look at long term incarceration the grieving process cuts much deeper into the lives of everyone involved. Loss of family, a loved one, a career, finances, and self worth equal multi-level grief with possible long term processing and recurrence.

Like it or not, when a family loses someone due to incarceration their grieving process is just as severe and painful as someone who has lost a loved one due to accident, disease, or death. I know this is not going to be a well-accepted observation but it is evident and obvious to those who are going through the loss process.

I understand that the loss of a loved one by death is a very painful process. I have been through that many times personally and professionally. As the saying goes, "been there done that!" and no matter how many times I've been through this scenario each one is just as painful, depressing, and debilitating as the first.

I've had individuals who became extremely angry with me for equating the death of a loved one to long term incarceration and I understood their anger.

However I have to point out that even though the loved one who is incarcerated can still be visited and is still alive, the loss of that individual's freedom effects everyone connected to him or her. It is the loss of the freedom to hold, love, and converse, argue, laugh, and/or sleep with that person that becomes so painful.

As with any loss, the burden falls on the shoulders of those on the outside that are now responsible for all of the financing, cooking, cleaning, child rearing, family responsibilities, etc.

As when death takes a loved one, it's the loss of the individual as well as their 50% of the partnership that makes us feel empty and hopeless. As any grief counselor will tell you, the survivor has to face the world alone. Holidays, birthdays, graduations, marriages of the children, and the rest of life's joys are now spent alone.

How do you explain to someone that the person they love can no longer attend a special occasion because they are incarcerated? It doesn't matter how small or big the crime may have been; it is still a difficult situation and a very empty existence for the family outside the walls. Even society may turn their backs on those grieving when they discover it is due to incarceration.

The families of death row inmates experience issues that have for too long been neglected by society, ministers, counselors, and clini-

4

cians alike. It doesn't require much thought to realize that these people have needs and that there is a general lack of support for the incarcerated and their families.

Disenfranchised grief leaves the inmate's children, families, and friends in a state of confusion dealing with the circumstances surrounding the execution and puts the family members outside the current accepted methods for working through grief.

It may sound very simplistic but my experiences have shown a little bit of creative thinking can go a long way when working with death row inmates and their families. Be willing to switch and change things up. There is no set step-by-step process in the field of grief management so be willing to explore and improvise. Things can change several times while waiting for the execution and each change of schedule could very well be a setback to all of the work you have already accomplished.

Why Worry About An Inmate's Grief?

This book is neither for nor against the death penalty and I don't wish for it to be used for any kind of political stance. I know from experience there are many individuals who have very strong ideas about this situation and everyone has a right to their own opinions about the incarcerated and the death penalty.

My dream with this book is that anyone dealing with incarceration achieves a better understanding of the grieving process and the benefits of working through these issues.

When it comes to working with the incarcerated all of my grief training had to be very flexible, and sometimes I had to do the opposite of what I was taught. Working with inmates, I soon realized that the grieving process began with the first court appearance and continued throughout the trial and sentencing.

I quickly came to the realization that it is not everyday I would get to work with someone who knew the exact date, time, and method of their death. Even when everything seemed to be in working order for the inmate and all the families involved, a change in the execution, for whatever reason, can set all of your work back to the beginning and you find yourself at square one.

Now everyone, including the family of the victim, had to go back to their everyday life and prepare to begin the process all over again.

This included rescheduling time off work, changing family plans, transportation time, re-booking hotels and travel. Also included are the financial strain and the guilt associated with wanting the whole thing to be over with. Sometimes closure can take ten to twenty years or may never occur at all.

Section One

Basics of the Grieving Process

Chapter 1

What is the Grieving Process?

There are literally thousands of websites and books that cover grief and bereavement issues.

The grieving/bereavement process is a natural and healthy reaction to the loss of someone or something that you love. Some individuals call it a broken heart but most often it is characterized by extreme mental anguish.

A person who is grieving a loss may believe that in time they will no longer miss a deceased person. But this is not true. If the deceased is someone they truly love they will always miss that individual. The TRUTH is that over time the pain of missing that person will ease and with a little bit of work the memories will be of happier times and not of the tragedy of the loss. This does take time and the pain can resurface when least expected.

Besides the loss of a loved one there are many different types of losses--the loss of a pet, divorce, loss of a job or career—these too can trigger grief and the pain associated with it. These losses may be triggered by memories associated with anniversaries, special days within the year, holidays, and birthdays.

Generally grief is easy to recognize and may be either physical, emotional, and in some cases both at the same time. They may experience any or all of the following:

- Ongoing sadness
- Denial
- Disbelief
- Shock
- Emptiness or Loneliness
- Loss of appetite
- Loss of or the fear of sleep

- Always feeling tired or may tire easily
- Obsession with the loss
- Anhedonia is the loss of interest or pleasure in activities.

Some of the most difficult feelings to cope with are the feelings of anger and/or guilt. Both are quite common but greatly misunderstood by the surviving individual. In cases of murder or suicide, anger may explode amongst family members due to guilt and these emotions can surface over and over again during the grieving process.

Grief Types Include:

- *Uncomplicated or normal grief.* All the healthy responses to a major loss would be considered normal grief.

- Working with a terminal illness diagnoses, divorce, sentencing of an inmate is what many professional counselors call *anticipatory grief.*

- *Anniversary grief* is the responses that can occur following, or anticipating, reminders of the loss, such as birthdays, holidays, anniversaries, or other very personal days. It is import that people understand that anniversary grief is not necessarily a setback in the grieving/recovery process.

- *Traumatic grief* or commonly called *Complicated grief* occurs when grief becomes disabling, intense, or chronic. This is believed to be the process of grief that could lead to major depression, symptoms of possible post-traumatic stress disorder and could include nightmares and/or flashbacks. Even though the American Psychiatric Association does not recognize Complicated Grief the National Institute of Mental Health (HIMH), states that ten to twenty percent of people grieving the loss of a loved one may experience Complicated Grief.

Chapter 2

What are The Stages of Grief?

The Stages of Grief are common emotional feelings associated with loss. Some individuals may experience all or just a few of these but the thing to remember is that they do not always happen in this order and you may experience some of these feelings more than once. However, what you are feeling is natural and over time you CAN recover from loss.

SHOCK

As with any loss there comes the feeling of shock and disbelief. Some individuals may express their shock without tears or emotions. Many times they may experience denial and the inability to accept what has happened. The most common expression I have heard from the people I have worked with over the years is "numb".

As time passes you will be able to express your emotions, although some people may go through a prolonged stage of shock whereas some adapt quickly and express their emotions immediately. Once again, there is no absolute guideline in working through grief. Accepting emotions as you experience them is the healthy process we all strive for. Give yourself time and give yourself permission to grieve.

PREOCCUPATION

When my sister was killed by an automobile in 1968, I was flown home by the U.S. Navy. I was only nineteen years old and she was six years old. As the only son of a divorced family I divided my time among my mother, my father, and the hospital where my eight year old sister, who was injured in the same accident, was convalescing.

After getting out of the limo and walking to the gravesite, I started to cry. My aunt hugged me and told me NOT to cry because I had to be a man and be strong for my mother. As she requested, I immediately stopped crying. I had no idea that shutting off the tears would lead to such a deep rooted pain that would take over a year of therapy to get through.

It is imperative that both men and women acknowledge their feelings and express their pain. I know from my own experience what can happen if you try to suppress your feelings. If I would have been able to share my feelings, I could have put closure to most of my pain in a healthy way and felt closeness with my family. By suppressing my feelings, I felt alone and isolated and that turned into anger against my family who were still mourning the loss of their youngest child. I became preoccupied with fantasies of how I could have saved her life had I been home instead of in the military.

Finally I met with a Navy therapist who explained to me there was nothing wrong except that I never had a chance to grieve. His advice was for me to return home without letting any of my family know; go to the cemetery and spend as much time as I needed at my sister's grave and give myself permission to cry, sob, wail, curse, or whatever it would take to heal my heart and let the grief out.

Sounds too simple doesn't it? But it worked! I don't remember how long I was at her grave or how long I cried; all I remember is when there were no tears left I felt like the weight of the world had been lifted from my shoulders.

Don't get me wrong, I still grieved for my baby sister, but I was able to go on with my life and was no longer crippled by grief. Even today, some 45 years later, I still remember her and some days when I think of her I smile and some days I still shed a tear. That's healthy grief!

Remembering someone who has passed away does bring hurt, but it diminishes over time. Instead of crying uncontrollably when I think of her now, there may be a tear, but typically I grin remembering something cute or stupid that we shared those many years ago.

The Symptoms of Grief

Physical and emotion stress may come in waves. The common physical distresses are as follows:

- Sleeplessness
- Tightness in the throat
- A choking feeling
- Shortness of breath
- Deep sighing
- An empty hollow feeling in the stomach
- Lack of muscular power
- Digestive symptoms and poor appetite
- Substance abuse
- Domestic violence
- Simple aches and pains
- Trouble concentrating

Children and adolescents experience the grieving process differently and may have different signs and symptoms while grieving.

- Withdrawal from friends
- Decline in school performance
- Unrestrained, aggressive play
- Refusal to attend school
- Asking questions about or imitating what was lost.
- Playing games about death or dying.
- Reverting to earlier behaviors such as bedwetting, baby talk, thumb sucking.

Grieving adolescents may experience these symptoms for an extended period of time. Some may turn to drugs, alcohol, or sexual activity in response to grief. If any adolescents express thoughts of severe depression or suicide while grieving, seek immediate professional help for that child!

HOSTILE REACTIONS

Some individuals respond to grief with a great deal of anger in situations that would not have bothered them before. These sudden outbursts of anger can be very surprising and very uncomfortable for the individual and those around them. This type of hostile reaction can make individuals feel as if they are going crazy and losing their mind. This anger can be directed at anyone at anytime including God and the loved one who has just died.

Feelings of anger and hostility can compound the feelings of guilt. Not understanding when or where the anger may surface brings about a large weight of guilt and non-controlability.

Individuals may accuse themselves of negligence in the death of the loved one--such as what they could have, should have, would have done but didn't. These hurts can pop-up in grief and may be associated with a lot of anger. This guilt is normal and should pass with time.

Feelings of hurt or hostility may be experienced toward a family member or friend who for various reasons does not provide the emotional support the grieving person is expecting from them.

It is important to understand that anger and hostility are normal. Do not try to suppress these feelings! At the same time, it is very important to understand and direct your anger towards what you are really angry at--the loss of the person you loved. It is OK to be angry at this person.

16

WITHDRAWAL

Individuals must accept the fact that during the grieving process they will experience withdrawal and depression. These are normal emotional reactions while grieving. With such a loss comes the disruption of their daily routine If an individual lives alone, lives a long distance from their family, or has little family contact these feelings can be intensified. Such feelings are normal and should pass with time.

Along with social withdrawal comes depression. Your whole world now seems like a bad dream and life doesn't seem the same. It is important to realize that life isn't, and won't be, the same after any kind of loss. You will experience moments of total despair, hopelessness, unbearable loneliness, and may experience

the feeling that nothing in your life is important any more or life has lost what value you held for it.

Working with clients over the years, I learned that a good sign of recovery was when they said the deceased would "come back and kick my butt" if I didn't start having a social life again, or they expressed similar thoughts.

It's important to accept your loss as real. Our first impulse is to deny our loss. Since we have a brain to think things through there are times we can intellectually understand the physical loss but still fail to accept the loved one is really gone and is never coming back.

Reaction to loss is as diversified as people are themselves. Some may travel, put in extra hours at work, or over extend their volunteer hours with the thought as long as they remain busy the loss won't be as difficult. Some idealize the loved one by refusing to allow negative thoughts about the love one enter their minds or turn to alcohol or drugs to deaden the pain.

LIVING WITHOUT

When we are grieving for the loss of a loved one it is important to realize we are grieving for a part of our lifestyle lost along with the deceased or the one incarcerated.

In relationships the wife, husband, spouse, life partner will miss them physically and emotionally as well as the loss of their friendship and support, conversation, and that soft white background noise that was always there. This could take a few months to sink in but it does happen.

We suddenly miss the companionship and the love, movies, walks in the park, long drives, or sitting quietly holding hands. As time goes on we begin to realize more of the little things now missing in our lives which can definitely compound the grief.

Grieving the loss of shared activities and life experiences can feel as painful as grieving for the person. It is at these times we feel our lives are emptier and this is natural and an important part of the grieving and healing process and why we need to shift our focus to family, friends, and activities.

Chapter 3

Myths and Facts about Grief

MYTH: It's important to be "strong" in the face of loss.

Fact: I told my story earlier in this book about the loss of my youngest sister and how as a young man I was told to be strong for the family. Whether one is male or female, feeling sad, frightened, empty, or lonely are normal responses to loss. Crying doesn't mean an individual is weak. Not crying does not mean you don't have a heart. People will react in many different ways.

Men may find the process they need for healing by being in the garage, woods, fishing, walking, and being alone. He may feel the need to build something or more likely to tear something apart and rebuild it. This is normal healing for many men. Men tend to need alone time to balance out their feelings and mentally create a plan of understanding and acceptance.

Women on the other hand may seek quiet time with another female friend or with family members. Again the difference in the sexes is just as different in the grieving process and recovery. Showing your true feelings can help the family and you recovery in a healthy way.

MYTH: Ignore the pain and you will heal faster.

Fact: Repressing or trying to ignore your pain and keeping it from surfacing will only make it worse in the long run. Ignoring your pain prevents you from real healing and it has been proven many times the best way to handle grief is to face it and actively deal with it.

MYTH: No tears, no grief, no loss.

Fact: This couldn't be further from the truth. Even though crying is a normal response to grief it is not the only method of dealing with grief. Different cultures, religious beliefs, family traditions, all play a part in the way a person grieves. It doesn't mean they don't feel the pain as deeply as others only that they have other ways of manifesting it.

MYTH: A year is enough so get over it.

Fact: The length of time it takes for a person to recover from grief differs from person to person. There is no right or wrong time frame for grieving, so to grieve healthily, take the time you need. Always remember however that an over extended period of time could be dangerous to your mental health.

MYTH: Moving too fast shows disrespect for the one you lost.

Fact: Forgetting and moving on are two different things entirely. Just because someone is creating a new life doesn't mean they can't keep their loved one's memory as part of their new life. Moving on means people have accepted their loss and their grief is healing naturally. Some may find the strength they need to move on by taking back their life as a sign of respect for the one they have lost.

MYTH: It's better to listen than to talk about the situation.

Fact: Yes, there may be times when just having someone present and sitting in silence is just what the person needs. Then there are times the person who is grieving may want and need to talk about their feelings of emptiness. By talking they are able to express their feelings of loss and emptiness.

Being there to bring up the subject can make it easier for them to talk about it. If you attempt to engage them in conversation and they are not willing, give them a little more time and let them know you are always available to listen.

You can take certain steps to help others cope with their grief by listening honestly, shopping for groceries, running errands, volunteering to do some yard or house work, laundry, or any other day to day activities that could help lighten the duties the grieving person may feel they just can't do at a given time.

Be careful of giving empty comments which could do more harm than good to a grieving person. Comments such as "They're in a better place"; "Their in God's hands now", "At least they're not suffering anymore" are terms meant to help but most commonly make the grieving person feel even worse.

Telling a child or teenager the deceased is in a "better place" could trigger suicidal thoughts so the child could be with the deceased in "that" better place.

Be careful of talking about God's intentions. Telling a child God called for the deceased and wanted them to have a better life in the hereafter could make the child hate God for not choosing them in addition to or in place of the deceased.

If you are not sure how to bring God into the conversation then don't. Give the child time to ask about God later in their grieving process and be careful not to make them hate or fear God.

Chapter 4

When to Seek Help

According to the American Psychiatric Association approximately 25 to 35 percent of people may develop severe depression after a major loss.

It is important the grieving process not be confused with serious mood disorders. When professional help is needed an evaluation by a physician or mental health professional may be needed to rule out other conditions.

According to "your total health" website (http://yourtotalhealth.ivillage.com) there are several symptoms of depression which do not typically occur in normal grief. When these are noted in people who have experienced a major loss, a psychiatric evaluation may be recommended:

- Suicidal Ideation. Grieving people may have a passive wish to "join" the deceased loved one, but do not normally dwell on the concept of their own death or exhibit suicidal behavior.

- Psychosis. People who are grieving may see reminders of their loss in many places, but do not normally develop delusions, or hallucinations involving the loss.

- Severe loss of self-esteem or functionality. Grief is often accompanied by some degree of functional impairment or feelings of reduced self-worth, but these are not normally severe.

- Psychomotor retardation. Significant slowing down of thought processes or physical activity does not tend to occur in normal grief.

Some other physical symptoms may include: Exhaustion, muscle tightness or weakness, body pains, fidgety restlessness, lack of energy. Insomnia, sleeping too much, disturbing dreams, loss of appetite, overeating, nausea, "hollow stomach", indigestion, intestinal disorders like diarrhea, excessive weight gain or loss, headaches, short of breath, chest pressure, tightness or heaviness in the throat.

Chapter 5

Taking Care of Yourself

During the time of crisis and grief a large majority of the population believes that taking care of you is selfish and not accepted as a healthy sign of recovery. They couldn't be further from the truth.

While grieving for a lost loved one the best thing you can do is to take care of you. You must learn to exercise control over your own life and the lives of any children who may be involved.

As numb as you may feel, you do have control over your own actions, activities, life, and choices. I cannot stress enough the importance of gaining a sense of control and confidence.

The following are a few suggestions for taking care of yourself and your life. The order in which they are listed is not important. The importance lies in picking the one you think you have the strength to start.

Tips in taking control of yourself:

1. Never stop Laughing! One of my most popular workshops is "Let's Laugh at Stress – A Holistic Approach". Laughter has been proven over and over again as a natural healing medicine. Laughter brings oxygen to the blood stream assisting in muscle relaxation. It produces endorphins, the body's natural pain killers, and laughing changes your expectations and can give you a whole new attitude on life.

2. Relaxation Activities such as ten to twenty minutes a day of relaxation down time. A massage can get your body to relax. Meditation gives your mind a chance to clear and refocus. Stretching exercises, such as yoga, will give you a sense of peace and relaxation.

3. Rest, Food, and Nutrition. Rest is very important in the time of grief. Rest has been proven to be a stress-buster and helps to energize the mind. Food and good nutrition help to re-energize the body. Combining all three help you feel better physically and will translate into how you feel emotionally.

4. Journaling is the process of writing down your current emotions and has been proven to be very therapeutic. You don't have to be a professional writer to journal, simply write down what you are feeling; it's as simple as that.

5. Take time to do something which gives you simple pleasure. Listening to music, take in a movie you've wanted to see, gardening, taking walks or anything else which can give you simple pleasure.

6. Faith or spirituality for inspiration and enlightenment. It is normal for many people to feel embarrassed about going back to church or a spiritual group if they haven't been there for awhile before the loss. Your faith or spiritual group is just what you may need at this time and I'm sure there is no need for embarrassment.

7. Support group sharing with a group of peers can help. For some, support from family or friends is all that is needed. This can help them talk through their stressful times and it's a way to have their feelings acknowledged and confirmed. Others may require support groups.

8. Buy CDs or books on coping with grief, stress management, or self-help. At the end of this book I list books, videos, and CDs which may assist you.

9. Accept help! Accept support from a group, family, or friends. When people offer assistance they might have suggestions that worked for them and it is a very good way to interact and share in the grief.

Chapter 6

Helping Someone Who is Grieving

There are several different ways you may help someone who is grieving. The following is a list of suggestions which do not have to be followed in any order:

- Help by trying to put regrets into perspective
- Suggest putting together a ritual
- Help clean out the loved one's things but use the time to reminisce
- Talking can help recall good times
- Urge the person to seek out a faith community or professional grief counselor
- Discuss the possibilities of a support group
- Don't be afraid to have a good time or to share laughter
- Assist with shopping, cooking, or writing thank you notes
- Plan for difficult times
- Share words of encouragement
- Stress the importance of taking care of their own health
- Be patient because grief will take time
- Sometimes simply sitting in silence can be of great comfort

Chapter 7

Grieving In A Healthy Way

As a minister who has worked with individuals who have lost loved ones, I want to share some basic information:

- Understand that there is no way to avoid the physical and/or emotional pain that comes with grief. This is especially true for men. Not letting yourself experience the pain can lead to physical symptoms and prolong the grieving process.

- Grieving for a loved one includes grieving for a part of you that is now lost. The loss can affect your life every time you come home to an empty house or the times there is no one there to talk with. Know with healthy grieving eventually comes acceptance.

- Learn to cherish memories, but be careful not to let them control every aspect of your new life.

- You may feel you are being disloyal by enjoying a new life without the loved one. Allow yourself to have these feelings but again do not let them control what you want in the future.

- When tragedy hits, it is normal not to want to accept the loss. Even though as humans we can understand the loss it isn't the same as accepting the loss. The first, and possibly the hardest step, is to accept your loved one is no longer a part of your everyday life.

- One of the most common questions I get from clients who are in the grieving process is "What do I do with the love I have for the individual?" This is a difficult time but it is extremely important to understand because you have lost a loved one doesn't mean you will stop loving them.

- When a memory pops into your head–and it will–embrace the memory with love and know you are still loved in return.

- Create a "place" where you can keep your memories. It can be something physical like a box, photo album, or a special place in the back yard, and for those who are spiritual when you have a memory tuck it into your heart space.

Section Two

Alcohol/Drug Recovery Grief

In the following chapters I will explain the grief and loss process of individuals in drug and/or alcohol treatment. Many people incarcerated may not realize they are experiencing grief during recovery treatment.

Individuals who are serving a court ordered treatment program will experience grief due to losing freedom, income, relationships, possible loss of custody of their children, and--the hardest loss of all--their self-respect.

Many of you reading this book may feel what those in recovery are experiencing isn't important because it's what they deserve and the result of their own self-destructive nature. Again this book intends no political statement but just looks inside individual grief experiences.

For counselors, case workers, and family members it is important to the client's recovery to understand the grief experience of each and every client.

Many of these individuals are just your average hard-working Joes who didn't expect to be in a recovery program and who are thrown into a whirlwind of unexpected change and disorientation after being arrested, going through the court process, and the sentencing.

It is common knowledge people during financial downfalls turn to alcohol or drugs to help relieve the pain. This has been the case throughout history.

They do not understand how this happened to them and the unexpected results that come from their self-destructive activities. Many individuals I have worked with over the last twenty plus years never in their wildest dreams thought they would wind up incarcerated. They did not consider their drinking or drug use any more then recreational and used the old excuse "Well everybody else I know does it so why am I being punished?"

The law is the law and when you break the law you are going to serve the time. I'm not talking about career criminals as much as I am talking about your co-workers, neighbors, family members, and possibly you!

Chapter 8

Alcohol and Drug Recovery Grief

Grief and loss start simply with the realization those red and blue lights behind you mean there is going to be a very uncomfortable change in your lifestyle. All of us have seen on TV the look of shock of those being arrested for being under the influence.

One client I worked with explained it this way: "When the red and blues came on I knew I was in serious trouble. Never in my wildest dreams did I think I was that loaded and would be pulled over. I mean there have been other times I felt more messed up than this time, so why now?"

"I just had a couple (drinks and/or joints) with some buddies after work like we always do so I didn't give it much thought."

"But man let me tell you once the red and blues came on I realized just how messed up I really was and I don't care what people say it doesn't sober you up quick enough to avoid being arrested!"

"Sitting in the back of the cruiser the reality of what was happening really hit hard." "How was I going to explain this to my boss, let alone my spouse and family? Financially things are really hard right now and I can't afford this!"

I can't remember how many times I have heard this same story but as a minister/counselor I have to bite my tongue and keep myself focused on the immediate situation and do my best not to pass judgment. Many have been lucky enough never to have been pulled over while under the influence and there are more of us who have been in this situation than we want to admit.

I have been fortunate to have clients who were willing to share their experiences and the following is what many of them had to say:

If you have not had the experience of being handcuffed in the back-seat of a police car it is difficult to understand the rush of emotions you experience. Many reported they sobered up enough to realize just how much trouble they were in and if they could live that night over never would have gone out drinking with their friends in the first place.

Many of them expressed the embarrassment of simply standing on the side of the road praying no one they knew would drive by and see them handcuffed or in the backseat of the police car.

Then you're faced with the realization of having to call someone who would hopefully bail you out without having to call your husband, wife, lover, or partner.

Just how much fear (followed by anger) is your loved one going to experience when they get the call? How are you going to explain why, despite your financial problems, you were out partying and how this is going to push your financial problems over the edge?

The unexpected legal expenses and loss of income due to a court ordered recovery program can be very devastating to anyone's budget. Even a ten-day program can ruin a budget which could take months to recover from let alone the possibility of losing your job.

Treatment programs are not free so now you have the added cost of the recovery program, court and lawyer fees, loss of income, major problems at home, possible loss of your job, and a criminal record that could affect any possible future employment or promotion. No matter how low they may have been feeling it isn't nearly as low as they are going to feel now.

We've all heard the old adage of "I'm not an alcoholic, I'm a social drinker!" Whatever the motives are for drinking or doing drugs they can come with a very heavy price tag.

Chapter 9

Grief During Treatment

Let's take a walk into a 120-day treatment program to better understand the grief and loss process. Most of these programs are court ordered, meaning an individual has already been incarcerated for being under the influence. It doesn't matter why or how much but simply there was enough evidence to cause an arrest.

Loss of self-respect: Standing in a court room where every detail of your arrest is being repeated can be extremely embarrassing and humiliating. With today's technology not only does everyone get to hear about your case but they will also be able to see you on video.

As you stand before the judge you feel the eyes of your family and loved ones behind you. You know in your heart the only question on their minds is how did this happen. Why did this happen? What's going to happen next?

You state your case and ask for leniency and pray for the best. If you're lucky you may catch a break but more likely than not you are going to get some jail time, the choice of entering treatment, or both.

You stand there waiting to hear the verdict and it is unbelievable the number of thoughts that will go through your mind. It seems to take forever when in reality it's only a couple of minutes.

You're thinking maybe they will let you off or worst case scenario maybe the weekend in jail. But to your surprise you hear the judge order you to attend a 120-day treatment program.

You grab a quick look at your loved one and all you can see is the tears and fear in their eyes. Those whom you love most have to take care of each other and you will only see them on scheduled visitation days.

Sitting in your cell waiting for transportation to the recovery center you find yourself desperately trying to adjust to what has just happened to you. You pray to God the men you will be spending the next 120 days with are a lot more civil than the ones you have been with in the local or county jail.

Now you're sitting in a transport with wire cages over the window. Going down the highway you see the everyday things in life passing you by that you never paid attention to until now.

You think about your home, your favorite chair, watching TV, munching out of the refrigerator during commercial breaks, going to bed when you want, having control over the thermostat, nice hot showers, and the list could go on and on but this is the reality of loss.

The ride seems to take forever as so many thoughts go through your brain you start to get a headache. The silence on the transport is made worse by the realization all you can do is go along for the ride and try to come out on top of the situation.

You arrive at the treatment center and you are feeling ashamed of being in jail stripes and even a little scared not knowing what's next. Just what is your life going to be like for the next 120 days? Are you going to be able to make it? And just how in the hell did you wind up here in the first place?

So this is what your life has come too! Zebra stripes, chores, and your whole life on someone else's schedule. How low can you feel!

There are many levels of loss, self-esteem, possible employment, and even worse is the possibility of the loss of family or partner.

The individual incarcerated will face many different aspects of loss and bereavement even though they might not realize it as it happens.

However, many people forget the loss and bereavement will be felt by the families and relationships who are trying to survive on the outside.

Many of the incarcerated clients I have worked with complain about the lack of visits by the spouse, partner, and family. It is important the incarcerated client realize without them being home to assist with everyday duties it is not always easy for those on the outside to drop everything for a visit.

Whenever one is incarcerated for any period of time those on the home front are serving the same sentence and can begin to feel over-whelmed.

Once the realization hits the inmate they will have yet another level of grief and loss to deal with in the deep feeling of failure as a pro-vider, mother, father, son, daughter, spouse, partner, employee, or employer.

For counselors it is important to understand these many levels of grief and bereavement can cause the client or inmate to react with anger and hostility without knowing why.

For women this is especially difficult since the inner workings of motherhood come to the surface of their emotions and the guilt is compounded with extreme feelings of failure.

Women who are incarcerated have the same issues surrounding grief and bereavement while being incarcerated as any man would. But incarceration will cut deeper into the female psyche if the inmate has children.

Chapter 10

Working Through Grief in Treatment

Grief is the natural emotion people experience following any major change in their familiar lifestyle such as illness, death, divorce, or retirement. Recovery from alcohol, drugs, sex and food addiction can cause feelings of grief and loss as they recover from the loss of a habit that has consumed so much of their life. Although these life experiences may not seem like grieving events, we grieve for all emotionally significant relationships in our lives including addictions.

Grieving is the normal reaction to loss all people experience at some point in their lives. How we react or cope with loss is completely individual. There is no way to measure the time or impact of the grieving process. The grieving journey is one of the most misunderstood emotional processes in contemporary life. We do whatever we can to avoid this natural life process.

Attempting to move through and cope with the intense emotional pain of grief in a healthy way puts most people in a deep state of confusion and depression.

Many individuals try to seek and find comfort from the internet. They feel they don't have time for support groups, workshops, or counseling.

Many times these searches for support come up short and individuals in recovery feel a deep sense of isolation.

It is very important to learn how to deal with grief while in recovery and to move properly through the grieving process. Many who enter and complete treatment deal with unresolved grief that created a void which is extremely difficult to fill.

Let's look at recovering from any addiction as though it were a death of a close and long time "friend". The grief and bereavement you feel for your friend is the same grief and bereavement you feel when you are in recovery.

For example: Someone very close to you dies. The first thing you experience is emptiness in both your personal and social life. As you go through the grieving process you find yourself remembering all the wonderful times you had. All of the important occasions and holidays you shared

Every day you are reminded of the great times the two of you had. No matter what you do socially you can't help but remember all the laughter you shared. Many of the social activities you used to enjoy just aren't the same without your "friend" being there.

You miss weekend activities, or nights of sitting in the back yard and solving all of the world's problems. Without that special friend by your side life just isn't the same and you hurt and feel lost, lonely, and misunderstood.

Now let's say that close "friend" was your addiction. It is the same sense of loss and grief you would experience over the loss of a close friend. If your addiction has always been an important part of your life this can become a major difficulty. Everything you have done with family and friends in your life has been associated in some way or the other with your addiction "friend".

Addictive behavior is with you your entire life. Everything we have done in our adult life has centered on addiction and it is hard to enjoy life without it. This includes your sex life.

For many in the recovery process getting clean and sober is like re-enforcing the loss of the "friend" because most memories are centered around events where alcohol and/or drugs were present. Family affairs and social gatherings are where most of us learned addictive behavior, and it is hard to know how to function socially with out it.

In grief language, this is a major loss to our life. Individuals in this stage of recovery no longer know how to socialize or interact. As with the loss of a loved one we don't know how to have fun like everyone else and we feel cheated so grief sets in.

Grief and bereavement in a recovery setting is just as complicated and painful as the loss of a loved one. Many people will dispute this statement but it has been my experience that once they realize this they seem to get a clearer picture of how grief and bereavement works in a recovery situation.

In time resentment will abate. Once a client embraces grief, they can see how their life will improve. They may start feeling well physically, be mentally alert and friendships and relationships will once again blossom. The main thing is it is possible to have a stable and fun life without being high.

Chapter 11

Grief and Recovery

Much has been said and written about grief and recovery; however I need to repeat a few of those comments. Grief in recovery is often overlooked or denied completely. It is necessary for all professionals working in recovery to look, learn, and incorporate some grief education as a foundation for their recovery programs.

Without some training and education in grief and bereavement many recovery programs are doomed to failure. Yes professionals can give a person in recovery many tools to assist them in their recovery program but without fuller understanding of human emotion these individuals will relapse.

When individuals relapse they blame others around them, or the recovery program was not directed to their needs, or their addiction was just too strong to resist.

All of these are justified but the unifying thread among them is the human capacity for self destruction combined with a denial or ignorance of the grieving process.

Grief and bereavement issues affect each and every one us at some time. It is part of our DNA to struggle against any threatening and uncontrollable emotion   It is part of our ancestral flight or fight mechanism and even today we can not avoid this most deeply imbedded human characteristic.

How we react to grief is learned from our families. Many of our family traditions are based on fear (in many forms) and not on understanding. So on to looking at long-term incarceration and grief.

Section Three

Grief in Long-Term Incarceration

Chapter 12

Grief in Long-Term Incarceration

Comparing Women & Men Behind Bars

There is very little research on women behind bars. Neither the rehabilitation of nor the collecting of information about women behind bars is a priority in the United States.

Obviously, imprisonment for women will be more difficult because women prisoners are more likely to have children who were living with them prior to their being sentenced. There is no stronger bond than that between a mother and her child which adds to the level of grief occasioned by separation.

Women will experience all of the tell-tale signs of grief that are discussed blow for the men, but not being with their children will take an enormous toll on women psychologically. Women not only have to deal with the separation but the chances are extremely high the prison will be located far from their children making visitation even more difficult.

The majority of women are sent to prison today due to substance abuse and other nonviolent crimes. Women in prison are likely to have been sexually assaulted and/or physically abused before going to prison. Drug addiction, prostitution, and theft could have been the standard method of providing for themselves and their children.

As with many men, women imprisoned have been raised experiencing domestic violence, sexual abuse, physical abuse, and alcohol or drug addiction demonstrating a family system model and promoting highly dysfunctional relationships.

Men identify their self-worth by what they have accomplished in life whereas women usually identify their self-worth by how others see them. When the family is dysfunctional the view they have of themselves is usually one of unimportance, worthlessness, and the inability to have a successful and productive relationship.

In today's society women are more prone to using polydrugs, cocaine, or meth as a way to have income or in the worst case scenario for self-medication due to family pressures such as being an unemployed, or under-educated, being a single mother.

Men on the other hand tend to abuse alcohol and drugs due to anti-social behavior. Drug abuse in the male society is about the thrill or due to peer pressures within their circle of friends and/or their role models.

When a woman is incarcerated she usually has left young children and will suffer deep-rooted grief based on separation from her family. As with the male inmate population, women will experience grief related to their self-perception as a failed parent.

Female inmates separated from their family and children may experience an intense feeling of shame associated with the separation. Since women are often the primary caregivers of their children they are now faced with the very real possibility of losing custody of their children, creating traumatic and compounded grief.

Within the female inmate population many women will experience physical and emotional pain due to the separation from their children.

As with men, incarceration of women can itself can elevate the experience of loss of material goods, finances, employment, and family which could become a primary indicator of future mental health problems.

Female inmates need gender specific programs if we are ever going to assist these women to reintegrate into society and become confident functioning women and role models.

I have worked with many inmates who were sentenced to long-term incarceration. Working only with male inmates I received a first-hand look at how those individuals survived and I was able to do a comparison of the layers of grief they experienced when going through the process.

A Distinct Grief In Incarceration

Long-term incarceration can leave an inmate in a land of forgotten-ness, the out of sight out of mind syndrome. The family slips into the "what did we do wrong?" syndrome—not always, but often.

As time passes, those on the outside continue with their lives and so do the survivors. Many inmates have shared with me the depression, hurt, and anxiety they feel when the time between visits began to noticeably lengthen. It's difficult for those "inside" to come to terms with the fact for those on the "outside" it is going to be more difficult to adapt to their new life. As with death, the pain of a loved one's incarceration diminishes with time.

The main difference is with a loved one being incarcerated there is the possibility for visitation but when those on the outside need companionship from the inmate they can not depend upon it. The visitation is always one sided and this can cause many layers of anger, frustration, and loss for all parties involved.

The option to visit doesn't always include physical contact. Depending on the facility and the crime committed the visitation may be through a window and talking with a phone. It may be in a general area where you may get a brief hug, but all of the long-term facilities have strict rules on limiting or disallowing physical contact.

So once again the person on the outside can not get basic physical and emotional support creating a heavier burden of anger and guilt for simply wanting the basics of human companionship.

Let's take a journey down the path to long-term incarceration. My first prison was a medium security prison and I was not prepared for the education I was about to receive.

I will not go into any details of crimes committed to protect the victims and their families, and I feel obliged to protect the families of the perpetrators since they were victims as well.

The crimes of the inmates I worked with ranged from possession with intent to sell, domestic violence, attempted robbery, grand theft auto, dealing in illegal weapons, and, as you shall see murder.

Life is a journey and we never know where it will take us. I never thought I would become a minister or grief counselor let alone a spiritual guide for someone on death row, assisting them and their family to prepare for an execution.

However, I learned early in my life never to question the good Lord about my life's journey.

I have always felt the desire to help others and give them the benefit of my life experience. It wasn't until I turned 50 that I sought a college education to achieve professional advancement.

All of this has influenced me to write this book including the suffering, anguish, and quilt I've experienced with the families of the incarcerated. Many of these families suffer in total silence not knowing where to turn for help in a society too quick to blame the whole family and not the individual for the crime committed.

Chapter 13

Levels of Incarceration

I think it is important to understand the different security levels of prisons and correctional institutions which can vary from state to state and county to county.

Security Level Descriptions:

1 = Minimum Security
2 = Medium Security
3 = Closed Security
4 = Maximum Security
5 = Administrative Maximum
6 = Super Maximum
(Some states break down levels to 1 through 9)

Level I - V prison housing - In general, the higher the security level, the more security risks a prisoner presents in terms of manageability or escape potential. **Level I** has a single security fence and does not house sex offenders; **Secure Level I** can house sex offenders and has full security perimeters; Secure Level I and above all have secure perimeters which include double fences, razor ribbon and a perimeter detection system; **Levels III** and above all have gun towers. Some prisons have more than one security level.

Minimum - A custody level in which the design and construction as well as inmate classification reflect the goal of returning to the inmate a greater sense of personal responsibility and autonomy while still providing for supervision and monitoring of behavior and activity.

Inmates within this security level are not considered a serious risk to the safety of staff, inmates or to the public. Program participation is mandated and geared toward their potential reintegration into the community. Additional access to the community is limited and under constant direct staff supervision.

Medium - A custody level in which design and construction as well as inmate classification reflect the need to provide secure external and internal control and supervision of inmates.

Inmates accorded this status may present a moderate escape risk or may pose a threat to other inmates, staff, or the orderly running of the institution. Supervision remains constant and direct. Inmates willing to comply with institutional rules and regulations may receive increased job and program opportunities.

Maximum - A custody level in which both design and construction as well as inmate classification reflect the need to provide maximum external and internal control and supervision of inmates primarily through the use of high security perimeters and extensive use of internal physical barriers and check points. Inmates accorded this status present serious escape risks or pose serious threats to themselves, to other inmates, to staff, or the orderly running of the institution. Supervision of inmates is direct and constant.

My stories are based on working with inmates that were incarcerated in security levels 1, 2, and 4. Even though several of the prisons where I have worked had all five levels, I did not work with any inmates in level 3 (Closed Security) or level 5 or 6 (Administrative & Super Maximum). It's not that I wouldn't work with inmates on those levels; I was never given the opportunity to do so.

Security Classification - The system used by the department to determine the appropriate prison security level of a prisoner. Levels range from I (minimum) to VI (super max). Generally, the prisoner's institutional behavior, length of sentence and escape potential determine the appropriate level.

Risk Prediction - Statistically validated factors predict the probability of a male parolee committing assault and property crimes while on parole. It has not been possible to develop predictive factors for women because of the small number involved. Using various factors the department considers potential risk—very high, high, medium and low for new violent crimes while on parole; and for property crimes—high, medium and low probability. Risk screening is used in determining eligibility for the state's Community Residential Programs and is incorporated within the department's security classification system.

Chapter 14

Why I Was Visiting a Prison

Back in the mid-eighties we moved into our new home in an older neighborhood. Many of our elderly neighbors had been living in this neighborhood most of their lives. One neighbor in particular was a very sweet and funny woman. Unfortunately it was her son who became my first prison contact.

He had been arrested and charged with possession with intent to distribute marijuana and received an eight year sentence for a nonviolent crime. His mother and father were too old to make the 90-mile round trip to the prison to visit their son and asked if I would visit him and be the messenger between him and his family.

Since I had known the inmate for a couple of years before his arrest I agreed to visit at least once a month if my job would permit. Little did I know what I was getting myself into!

They wrote him telling him to send me the paper work necessary for me to be added to his visitor's list. In order for a visit, I had to pass a complete background check, permanent address, place of employment, three personal contacts, and a great deal of time waiting to see if I had been accepted for visitation.

Once I was accepted, I had to write requesting a date for visitation on a weekend or weekday, morning or afternoon, and my secondary choice. Even after all of this there was no guarantee I would get my requested date for visitation.

I had to go through this several times before we could finally match my schedule with the prison visitation schedule. What a pain in the neck but the inmate had forewarned me this would happen. Once I had a couple of visits under my belt the process became a lot easier-- but not much.

All of this protocol had perked my interest in just how the prison system functions and what other kinds of visitation horror stories would other family members of inmates have to share?

I had yet to begin my journey in grief and bereavement counseling but I could already see the type of mental anguish the system was causing and I hadn't even been through the gates yet. This was going to be a very interesting journey indeed.

The drive itself was uneventful until I turned down the road to the prison. The cold concrete and brick buildings are surrounded by industrial fencing topped off with the infamous razor wire surrounding the whole compound. Some have watch towers, armed guards, not one but two or three rows of fencing and razor wire with roadways in between the fencing. It makes you question how anyone can survive in such an environment and this is just a minimum security facility. Why do non-violent offenders have to serve time in a minimum security prison?

You can't help but wonder what happened in someone's life to put them in such a place. But I had to accept I volunteered to do the visitation as a favor so I looked at it as a learning experience and nothing more. Little did I know what you may plan and what really happens are two separate matters altogether.

Once I was able to figure out how to get into the visitor parking lot I just sat in the car and watched everything that was going on. There were inmates in the exercise yard hanging around in groups; some were exercising, some just talking, and some just sitting alone.

Everything was just like you've seen on TV, or at the movies, but this was real, no actors, no camera, no lights, and no going home at the end of the filming. These were men whose lives somehow had gone terribly wrong and in one beat of the heart had made a wrong decision.

I tried to imagine just what to expect when I went through those security doors. I had no idea what I was going to be up against but could it really be so bad? I was about to receive my first lesson in not having any control over your own life and it was going to be a shocker.

Being a smoker at the time I decided to stand outside my car and have a cigarette as I took everything in. Little did I know this was a major violation of prison the rules. It was alright to smoke in your car but standing outside the car posed a threat to security standards and I was introduced to a security guard before my third puff. I must say he was not the friendliest man I had ever met but quickly came to the conclusion it was time for the good old "Yes Sir" and "No Sir" routine.

Ahh, there's nothing like the feeling of a warm greeting starting with, and I quote! "What in the f**k do you think you're doing fool?" "Get back in your car or get the hell out of here before I arrest your stupid ass!"

Bam, reality check, and I quickly replied, "Sorry Sir this is my first visit and I didn't know this would be against the rules, I apologize!" Thank God for my being raised in the "yes sir – no sir" environment. Then he informed me if I was going to smoke get back in my car until the time the doors were open for visitors.

I have to admit at this point all of my cool and balanced reasoning was out the window. Sweat was running down my armpits, my heart was going a hundred miles an hour; my brain hit the fight or flight scenario from our caveman beginnings. I wasn't sure if I was going to sit back in my car or drive off and all I remember is sitting in the driver's seat trying to decide whether to stay or to go?

If I could panic this easily in the parking lot what would it be like to be in a transportation van knowing you are being delivered to this facility and it would be home for the next five to ten years? It was time to bite the bullet and get in the visitation line and wait for the doors to open.

Chapter 15

My First Prison Visit

Standing in line I wanted to start a conversation with someone, any-one, who had experience with the visitation process. There was a small group of women talking and laughing together so I didn't want to interfere. There were several elderly couples in the line but the looks on their faces told me they were in no mood for conversation.

That's when a young woman behind me asked if I was the one yelled at in the parking lot? "Yep, that was me!" I told her and she started to laugh. This helped me relax a little and was an open door for a question and answer period. God bless this woman for she was gentle and kind and more than willing to talk.

She was visiting her brother and made the 145 mile round trip drive every two weeks for the last four years. Now that's dedication! I'm not at liberty to share her story since at the time we met I had no idea I would ever be writing a book on this subject.

I knew to leave everything in my car except my ID (but no wallet), visitation approval letter, cash for the vending machine, and nothing else. She gave me the following breakdown for visitation:

1. It was best to have a roll of quarters in a Ziploc baggie than to bring paper money due to the change or vending machines always running out of coins and unable to make change.

2. It was OK to bring in cigarettes but bring an un-opened pack rather than having the security guard spend time searching the open pack.

3. Be prepared for a longer wait than anticipated since what may be going on inside could create limitations on how many visitors could go in at one time.

4. Once you went through the screening area DO NOT under any circumstances go back out unless you were planning to leave the facility.

5. In small groups a security guard would escort you through the first locked down security gate. Once that security gate is closed and locked they would open the second security gate and let you into the holding area.

6. Always let your inmate know what day and time you will be visiting otherwise if they have to look for the inmate who could be on a work detail, you would have to wait until the next visitation which could be in the afternoon, the next day, or not at all that week.

7. Once you got your black light hand stamp and were let into the inmate visitation area find a table and quietly wait until the inmate had his body search and was permitted to enter the visitation area.

8. Inmates were not permitted under any circumstances to go to the vending machine and purchase drinks or snacks alone. They were not allowed to have contact with money. They could accompany the visitor to the vending area to let them know what they wanted to eat or drink then return to their table.

9. (This was during the time the prisons permitted smoking). If the inmate didn't have his own cigarettes you could give him one cigarette at a time out of your pack. Inmates were permitted to have matches but no lighters.

10. At the end of the visit you could not give the inmate cash, lighters, pens, paper, notes, cards, cigarettes, or anything else they did not have with them when they came into the room. Birthday cards and such could be given to the guard to search and the guard would give the card to the inmate once back in the secured area.

11. Jails and prisons have a strict dress code for visitors and any violation could suspend your visitation rights indefinitely.

12. Check with the jail or prison to find out the age limit for visitation. Depending on the degree of the crime, medium security, versus maximum security, versus death row all have different requirements and limitations on visitation of young people.

13. Anyone on probation or with a felony charge can under no circumstance s visit an inmate.

14. Possession of any type of illegal drugs, weapons, or things that could be used as weapons or items not on the visitation list could result in immediate arrest and being barred from visitation.

She shared all of this information with me which gave me the knowledge to make all further visits as easy as possible. Having a regular visitation schedule also gives the security guards a chance to get to know you by face or by name and it seemed to make entry a whole lot easier.

The easier you make it on the security guards, the easier you will make it for you and for the inmate as well. Like it or not, if you do anything to upset the security guards it will be taken out on the inmate in some shape or form.

Going through prison security is like going through airport security: emptying your pockets, taking off all jewelry, belts, removing shoes and jackets, placing all money, cigarettes, and lighters into the little plastic container before walking through the security scanning machine.

The major difference is once you have gone through this stage of security you were escorted through a big solid iron gate into the holding area. The area is approximately 12X12 feet and you wait until they have a limited number of visitors in the area: then they close the gate. I will never forget the sound of gate clanging shut.

Sure you've heard the same sound on TV or the movies but until you are standing right there it is a sound like you have never heard before, an trust me it isn't the friendliest of sounds.

Once the first gate is secured, they unlock the opposite side security gate to let you into another holding area. There you put your hand through a hole in the window and the security guard checks your hand stamp with a black light.

If your inmate has already cleared security, he will be sitting at a table waiting for you. If not you pick a location and wait until they finish their strip search and have him cleared for visitation.

My inmate had not been cleared when I entered the visitation area so I had a chance to sit and look around. I dare say 95% of the inmates I observed were men you could see any given day at work, school, grocery stores, soccer games, and even at your neighborhood church.

The other 5% were the type of men who really don't look like criminals but you somehow know not to make prolonged eye contact. Something in their eyes and body language tells you it wouldn't take much for them to explode into a fit of rage and possible violence.

My heart went out to those inmates who did have their children visiting. You could see the pain and embarrassment in the inmate's eyes knowing they would only be together for maybe an hour or two and then separated until the next visit.

Then the inevitable child's question, "Daddy when you coming home?!" I had never witnessed such a depth of regret for all involved including the inmate, spouse, and child as when "Daddy" tried to explain why he could not leave with them. Little did I realize this would be my first look into the world of grief and bereavement for the incarcerated.

Chapter 16

First Contact

Sitting at the table waiting for Bruce I had nothing else to do but watch everything going on around me. I sat watching the smiling faces on the inmates as they came into the visiting room searching for their loved ones followed by hugs and warm greetings.

When I saw Bruce his face lit up but I was still quietly shocked at how much his faced had aged. It seemed as if he had aged ten years in the short time he had been locked up.

I explained his folks were doing well even though his father had been diagnosed with early Alzheimer's and his mother's diabetes was taking its toll on her health. I really didn't want the visit to start on such a low note but I had to tell him the truth on why they weren't able to visit.

After a trip to the vending machine area we sat down for an in-depth conversation about how his life was going and what it was like in lockup.

Not being a big man I was concerned about all the horror stories I had heard about prison, so I just wanted confirmation for his parents he was doing OK.

He admitted he had already been in a couple of fights and even though he was not a violent man he explained if you didn't fight back it would cause more trouble than being in a fight. You have to stand up for yourself or everyone else would be coming after you.

He was getting along well with his cellmate and the two of them were watching each other's back whenever they could. In the six months he had been there things seemed to be settling into a regular routine and he was making all the necessary adjustments it takes for life behind bars.

He had seven and a half years to go and I promised him I would try to visit as much as my schedule would permit. His parents said they would try to make it up for a visit but I told him there was no way they would be able to visit in their current medical conditions.

His mother had her hands full taking care of his father and wouldn't be able to write him as much as she wanted but really looked forward to getting his letters.

This was when I realized he couldn't write home often because he didn't have money to buy the paper, envelopes and stamps. We both knew his parents were on a very limited income and couldn't afford to keep him supplied all the time.

Now I started to understand what kind of losses one would experience in prison. He knew he couldn't afford a TV but asked me to ask his folks if they could send him some money to buy a small CD player and head phones.

He explained with the head phones he didn't have to listen to all the "talk" on the cell block where he was living. He stated it was one of the hardest things to adjust to. All the yelling and screaming that took place between the cells and the different levels of the cell block were nerve wracking.

At times he said it was so loud and overbearing you just felt you wanted to scream your head off for everybody to just shut up. So loss of privacy, loss of quiet, and a little loss of sanity and he had only been there six months!

He told me he had been in and out of jail for minor offenses and really thought prison wouldn't be much different. He had never been so wrong in his life. Jail was a breeze but in prison you have to watch your back 24/7.

You take group showers, your toilet is in your cell where you and your cellmate live and sleep. Your whole life is now squeezed into a 5 foot by 7 foot cell with a bunk bed, sink, toilet, small window, and no privacy. You have to hold up a sheet for privacy when you are on the toilet.

He was waiting to get a job assignment so he would earn a little money to buy necessities such as soap, toothpaste, tooth brush, shampoo, and occasional snack food or soda. Again all the little things we take for granted on the outside you have to purchase on the inside and it's not cheap.

In prison you spend no more than you would spend on the outside but your income in prison may only be $10 to $20 a week. Stop and think about that for a moment. Just how many personal hygiene products, food, & clothing could you afford on $50 a month if that?

Some of you may be thinking: "Hey they put themselves in there so deal with it!" No matter how true this may seem, remember, these are non violent criminals and all they want is a little bit of dignity.

Common everyday things which are meaningless on the outside mean so much more when you don't have them. They know they messed up but they didn't expect the life awaiting them behind prison walls.

When you lay down to go to sleep tonight think of sleeping in a three-story tall tunnel filled with maybe 150 to 200 men, snoring, bodily sounds, moving around in the dark: creepy to say the least.

Now back to my first visit with Bruce. Listening to him talk about what he didn't have, I quickly realized I was in danger of becoming his Phone Company, bank, post office, and grocery store. I couldn't afford to support him and I knew his parents couldn't afford it either.

What was I going to tell his folks? No matter his crime he was still their son and they would make sacrifices to help him, so I realized I would have to limit some parts of Bruce's conversation and requests. I would help out when I could but I have to admit I was more concerned about taking care of his parents than him. Right or wrong his folks lived closer to me and were my first concern.

After visiting hours were over, I told him I would try to visit in two weeks. I would speak with his folks and see what we could come up with to help him out. Whatever we could do he would have to mail a list of what we could and could not purchase, how many of each item, box it up, and then ship it to him.

T-shirts, underwear, socks, personal care items, snacks, and food all had to be done by a check list. We just couldn't go out shopping. Certain colors were not permitted as were certain types of clothing and the number of purchases.

I would have no problem shopping for what he needed and boxing it up for shipment but it all had to be carefully weighed, packaged, and shipped according to the prison check list rules and regulations.

When I left the prison that day I remember sitting in the parking lot once again and trying to figure out just what happened in that short visit with Bruce. My whole outlook on life had taken a sharp and unexpected turn.

The ride home was full of memories of what I had just experienced and I knew in many ways my life was never going to be the same. All of these crazy unexpected emotions and I was only visiting for a few hours. How would I cope in a similar situation? Could my life take a wrong turn and could I end up serving a long prison sentence?

What and how could I tell his mother all these things without lying? How could I keep breaking her heart? Last but not least, would I be able to keep my promise and go through all of this again in two weeks or should I just bite my tongue and back out?

It's a decision I hope none of you ever have to make. If you are in this situation, remember it's all about giving and sharing love in the worst possible conditions.

I'm going to skip ahead five years since the visitations didn't change much over the years. Our next stop on this journey is what happens when a long term inmate loses someone at home and gets hits full force with powerless grief.

Bruce's father passed away and Bruce was not permitted to attend the funeral. Apparently he had gotten into a scuffle with another inmate and was put into the "hole" for his behavior. As I had said before you "either

fight for yourself or become a target by everyone on the block!" This isn't uncommon for prison but his timing couldn't have been worse.

I contacted the prison officials to let them know his father had passed and see what we could do to have Bruce attend his father's funeral. Even under normal circumstances he may not have been permitted to attend and being in the hole in a medium security prison wasn't helping either.

Now remember it had been five years since he last saw his father and now he was not going to be able to be at the funeral with his family, say goodbye to his father, or support his mother.

It's difficult enough when one loses a parent but to not be able to have the choice to attend the funeral is a major loss and the build up of guilt and depression can be debilitating.

Like it or not Bruce had to accept the fact that he was in a medium security prison and no one had put him there but himself. During the visitation I told him his father had passed and the hardest part for Bruce was to not cry in public.

Still not knowing what it is like to live in prison he had to explain to me even when an inmate loses a loved one (other than the loss of a child) anyone seen crying would be considered weak and vulnerable to attack.

In prison you can not display any weakness under any circumstances without the possibility of being seen as a target. Everything we think we know about the male psyche is so much different in a prison setting.

Displaying any type of emotion would be considered un-manly or feminine and a sign of weakness. It is not acceptable for any man in prison to so show emotions without being harassed by fellow inmates and sometimes even the guards.

All Bruce could do was keep the hurt and pain buried deep within him and not display any reaction to the news until he could hopefully find a place of solitude. Otherwise as I have mentioned before, the hurt and pain are going to get buried and could cause sever anguish or mental problems in his near future.

I promised him I would take care of his mother to the best of my ability and he needed to find a prison counselor who would help him through his current crisis.

I had done everything possible for Bruce and only time would tell how he would survive and recover from this situation.

Chapter 17

Unexpected Transfer

Another year had gone by and Bruce had been in front of the parole board several times but never succeeded in getting paroled. One of the realities for Bruce, as he put it, was if he had committed a violent crime he would have been paroled by now. However, it seems nonviolent criminals hardly ever get paroled and usually end up serving their complete sentence, or at least this is how Bruce saw it.

On one of my visits I was surprised to show up for the visitation only to discover Bruce was no longer at the prison. This would throw anyone for a loop. The prison officials explained to me he had been transferred THAT morning to a different minimum security prison several miles away. It seemed to me they should have contacted the family and let them know before the transfer took place.

I had to return home and tell his mother what had happened and wait until we heard from him on how, when, and where I could visit again. It took about a week before we received Bruce's letter and to our dismay we had to start the whole process of visitation all over again with a different prison with different rules and regulations.

The most upsetting part of his transfer was losing the small black and white TV, CD player with head phones, and a few other items that his parents had managed to provide him.

He couldn't take any of these belongings with him due to the risk of contraband which could be hidden in the compartments or the cost of transporting the items.

I don't care what they say about cost; it couldn't have been more expensive than having his family put out more money for another TV, head phones, CD player, etc. Of course we could purchase all of these at the new prison commissary by putting more money into his

73

prison account. His mother is living alone now and just doesn't have the money and feels like she is letting her son down yet once again, causing more guilt and grief because of the new rules and regulations.

On the home front things were not looking too good for Bruce's mother. She was losing her battle with diabetes and I didn't know how much longer she would be with us.

I had convinced her to let me have a front door key because I was tired of kicking in the door when she would call and be lying on the floor unable to get up. I was in the habit of checking on her every night, making sure she had something to eat, empty her potty chair, and wash her bed sheets, normally a son's job.

Once again I found myself in the middle trying to let Bruce know how she was doing without adding to his guilt about not being there for her.

She would give me money to shop for him but I would always sneak most of it back into her envelope when I could and never told her how much the items cost or what I had spent.

It took a month to get visitations straightened out with the new prison. I had to send proof his mother was too ill to visit and since I wasn't a relative, I had to go through the process of a background check, finger printing, etc.

I have to admit once the visitation rules were complete the visitations were more relaxed and we both had more freedom.

Unlike the last prison, which had a heavily barred visitation room, at this prison there was an outside area with picnic tables and a smoking area. By that time all of the jails and prisons had gone non-smoking inside the facility.

Bruce's attitude had improved greatly and I was able to assist getting him into therapy to work through his grief about being in prison but more about the grief of losing his father and not being able to attend the funeral in support of his mom.

Seven months into his therapy his mother passed away. The prison personnel had gotten to know me pretty well by then and when I called with the news I asked if I could skip the regular visitation routine and just drive up and give him the news face to face.

Not only did they agree to this but they had a Chaplain on standby waiting for me so he and I could take Bruce to a private area to share the bad news.

Speaking with the Chaplain while waiting for Bruce, he explained to me that unlike when his father had passed, Bruce would be able to attend his mother's funeral, if I was willing to do a lot of the leg work back home. Naturally I agreed and told him as soon as he sent me the information of what I needed to do I would start the procedure on my end and pray he could make the funeral.

The process wasn't bad; it just took lots of phone calls and making specific arrangements with the funeral home. Fortunately for me the funeral home had been through this before and was extremely helpful in assisting me in what needed to be done.

I told Bruce's family he would be able to view his mother but it would not be on the same day of the family visitation and funeral. None of his family would be permitted to see him or be with him at his mothers viewing.

The prison would furnish transportation to and from the prison and he would be under guard the whole time. Once at the funeral home they would secure the building and only the funeral home director, guards, clergy, and Bruce would be permitted to attend.

Once again the Chaplain was wonderful and did make arrangements so I could attend as support for Bruce and on behalf of his family. He was only permitted 30 minutes and it took a lot of talking but between the Chaplain and I we were able to get the guards to unhandcuff Bruce long enough to touch and kiss his mother goodbye and then they put them right back on his wrists.

I did the best I could to comfort Bruce as we stood next to his mothers' casket. The guards were very understanding and gave us a few minutes together so Bruce could grieve privately the best he could in the short amount of time he had.

It may not seem like much but it meant the world to Bruce to be able to hug his mother for the last time and not be handcuffed. A little bit of freedom for a lasting goodbye.

I could see the grief in his eyes when he thanked me for all I had done for her and his family and I knew he felt terrible for not being there in his parents' time of need and final hours.

Chapter 18

Farewell to a Friend

Bruce served his full eight-year prison term and returned to his parents' house. Now that he was out we could sit down and talk about just what it was like for him in prison.

Bruce said his reality of the pain he had caused his parents was never more obvious than on the day in court when he received his eight-year sentence. He stated the look on his parents faces was a look he would carry to his grave. It was the beginning of the grief and bereavement process.

Never in his wildest dreams did he believe he would ever hurt his family in this way. He had done a lot of youthful stupid things growing up but never believed he would serve so much time in prison nor put such a hardship on his parents.

He said he would never be able to repay me for the kindness and dedication I had shown his parents. The magnitude of guilt he felt knowing a neighbor had taken on all the responsibilities that by blood were his and because of youthful stupidity he couldn't meet.

At the time I hadn't any thoughts of becoming ordained or being a grief and bereavement counselor. I didn't have the education to be able to put his concerns to rest nor the ability to assist him in working through all of his grief.

After eight years in prison his life on the outside was more difficult than he had imagined. He had major issues in just finding work let alone good paying employment. If his parents had not left him their house he would have been living on the streets.

Consider your own life and what your income was in the 1980s. What was the cost of an automobile, groceries, gas, clothing, heating, or standard home repairs? Now think about going to sleep for eight years and waking up in today's financial market. Cultural shock? I believe so.

In 1980 Oreo cookies 15 oz. pack was only $0.99 cents, by 1988 a 20 oz. pack was $2.49. The average cost for a new car in 1980 was $7,200.00 where the average cost for a new car in 1988 was $15,400.00. The cost of a home in 1980 was around $68,700.00 whereas the cost of a home in 1988 was up to $91,600, a $22,000 increase in just eight years. Yearly mean income in 1980 was $21,063 and in 1988, $34,017, which means the cost of a home, jumped $22,000 in eight years but income only went up $12,954 dollars.

By now you understand how long term incarceration can bring on intense feelings of inadequacies, depression, loss of self-esteem, and loss of the ability to provide for one's family and lead to an inmate's desire to return to prison and a life they could better understand.

If you have children, find a picture of what your child looked like at the age of one. Now find a picture of the same child at the age of nine years old. How much of a change do you see?

Inmates released from long term incarceration quickly realize the small little bundle of joy they had left behind is now much older and very possibly not as interested in seeing "Dad" as the inmate is in seeing his child .

Bruce didn't have any children, yet he still suffered from grief and the loss of his own youth and, as he saw it, his inability to be a man.

All he could find were lower than minimum salary jobs. You just can't tell a prospective employer you just decided to take eight years off! Most of the jobs he was offered he couldn't take because his fellow workers would be users of the same substance that had him locked up in the first place. Being on parole was a no-win situation for Bruce.

It didn't take long for Bruce to hit rock bottom in self-esteem. We had many conversations about how he couldn't wait to get out and now that he was out he found himself wishing he was back in. At least in lock up he knew the rules and regulations required of him.

Now on the outside so much had changed he really didn't think he had a chance to survive in this new and expensive world. On his release from prison he knew he wouldn't be able to afford the things he wanted in life but he didn't realize he would have such a hard time simply surviving.

The last time I spoke with Bruce he was moving west where a friend of his owned a business. He didn't know how it would play out but he would have a job and thought there was a better chance there where no one knew of his incarceration.

Several months after he moved I received a letter informing me Bruce had passed away at the age of 31. It stated he had taken his medication before dinner, had a few beers before bed, and then consumed the same dosage before going to bed and died in his sleep from an overdose.

Was it an accidental death? I don't know. I wasn't there. Could it have been prevented? I do believe it may have been prevented with proper grief and bereavement counseling.

Chapter 19

First Visit Summary

Now that you've read this story I want you to go back to the beginning of the book and see how many of the following questions you can answer. There are no wrong answers so base the answers on what you feel and think about bereavement with the incarcerated.

1. How many of the general grief symptoms would apply to this story?

2. Under the grief types listed how many can you identify from this story?

3. What stages of grief would take place?

4. Can you identify how many myths could take place in this scenario?

5. If you were the parent of the inmate what steps would you take in taking care of yourself?

6. If you were the neighbor how would you have helped them in their grief?

Again there are no wrong answers but I want to give you the opportunity to think about how you would react if you were one of the characters in this story.

Chapter 20

Another Story

Here is another story I am permitted to share with you. I'll call this inmate 'Seth" since he was a tall, six foot four inch, thick framed but skinny country boy. Seth and I met while I was still working construction and we hit it off as friends immediately. He was a good hearted man, on the shy side, and easily intimidated.

One of the things that always troubled me was at least twice a month he would show up for work bruised with a black eye or busted lip. Sometimes he would have a limp in his walk and you could tell his spirit was really low.

I tried but could never get him to tell me what was going on, and he just didn't strike me as the bar fighting type. Actually I couldn't see him in any kind of fight.

Then one day he just didn't show up for work and no one knew what had happened or where he was. He didn't have a phone, or at least never gave out the number and only the owner of the company had his address but would not give it out. I didn't hear from him again for almost ten years and the reason might surprise you as much as it surprised me.

I had started a new career working at our local AIDS agency as a Risk Reduction Specialist and one day when I got home from work I was told a heavily tattooed big muscular man had stopped by looking for me. I didn't know anybody that had lots of tattoos let alone being very muscular in build so I had no idea who it could have been.

A couple of weeks later the door bell rang and when I answered the door the man standing there looked familiar but the face just didn't fit the body. I knew instantly it was Seth, but it looked like someone had cut his head off and put it on a completely different body.

Seth was now about 230 pounds of rock hard muscle and from the neck down every piece of exposed skin was covered in some amazingly detailed tattoo work. I just couldn't believe it was Seth.

Seth asked if he could visit for awhile and I invited him in for what turned out to be a three hour counseling session. Turns out Seth had been in prison for the last nine years and the story about his being incarcerated is one I'm sure will surprise and astound you as it did me.

When Seth and I were working construction together the reason he showed up battered and bruised so often was because of his wife. She was the batterer!

Now remember I am talking about the early eighties and back then society still didn't believe a woman would be the abuser in a domestic violence situation. Seth was tall and slender (about 135 to 140 pounds) and a very timid man personally.

There was no way in hell he was ever going to tell the men he worked with on a construction site he was being battered by his wife. His wife was no small woman by any means and as I looked back over the years I had no difficulty in visualizing her being able to kick just about any man's butt across the yard.

Seth's only concerns in life was making sure his children had a good clean home, clothes on their backs, and food on the table. Apparently his wife used this against him over and over and over again.

The last time she beat him he was protecting his children. By the time the police and emergency units arrived she had told him if he didn't go along with her story he would never see his kids again.

His kids meant the world to him and he would do anything not to lose them. The story she told the police: she was defending herself again from one of his brutal attacks and he had a history and police record of violence and attacking her.

The laws about domestic violence were starting to change and even the police report filed by both officers and the medic's stated he had to be hospitalized and she didn't have a mark on her. Nobody was buying her story and even though Seth confirmed her story the police decided to start their own investigation.

Because Seth supported her story he was put on probation and she filed a restraining order against him. He was not permitted to see his children or be anywhere around them without someone from children's services being with him when he visited with them.

After several court appearances the court dropped the restraining order but he was still on probation for five years and being on probation was the leverage she held against him. If he didn't do everything she demanded, she would report he had broken his probation and he would go to jail.

One evening not only was she starting to beat him again but for the first time Seth knew of she was starting to beat on the children.

Seth said he doesn't remember much after seeing her hit the kids, but apparently all those years of abuse boiled over and he tackled her to get her away from the children. This time it turned into an all out brawl. He was not backing down and he was not going to let her hurt the children.

He pushed her down and grabbed the children and put them in his pickup truck. He then went back inside the house to grab some clothes for him and the kids. Unbeknown to Seth after they had left court weeks before she had gone out to the truck and hid a large hunting knife in the glove box and a pistol under the driver's side of the truck.

Seth went back out to the truck and left with the kids to a hotel to figure things out. Of course his wife called the police and told them he had attacked her, kidnapped their children, and was armed and dangerous.

By this time the police had an idea of what was really going on, but had to look for Seth anyway, and of course they found him. After her report they had to search the truck for weapons and sure enough found the pistol and hunting knife which was in direct violation of his parole. Even though the police suspected it was a set up there was nothing they could do but arrest him on all charges.

This is what sent Seth to prison for 15 years but he was paroled for good behavior after 9 years. It was during those nine years in prison that he began working out and building up his body and obviously discovered the world of tattoos.

He was determined that no one would ever abuse him or his kids again. Looking at him after his release, you would understand why no one wanted to stare at him for too long. He looked as if he could just twist your head right off your shoulders and he probably could.

He had returned home to live with his wife and children. When I asked him why, he simply stated "hey that's where my kids are!" On his return home with his new physical appearance and attitude it seemed she had calmed down quite a bit.

Over the next four to five months we kept in touch and I was really happy for him since it appeared that his life was actually turning around. How wrong could I have been?

Seth didn't know his wife had been seeing another man while he had been in prison and his coming home had really messed up their plans. The man was introduced as his wife's cousin and since he and Seth both loved motorcycles they hit if off immediately. Little did Seth know his love of motorcycles would be his down fall?

One night the "cousin" called Seth and told him his motorcycle had broken down and he had to leave it on the side of the road. Since he was at work and it was starting to get dark, would Seth mind picking up his motorcycle and take it home where he would get it the next day.

Seth didn't think twice about it and picked up the motorcycle. You are probably thinking Seth should have known better by now but he was a trusting man.

You guessed it. The motorcycle didn't belong to the "cousin". It was a motorcycle he just saw on the side of the road on his way to work. Once Seth got home with it in the back of his truck his wife called the police and said Seth had stolen a motorcycle for parts and he was still on probation.

The down side of this story is being on probation Seth was sent back to prison to finish his original sentence meaning he had to serve the last six years. While he was in prison he was able to get a divorce and his parents got custody of the children. His wife and her "cousin" were found guilty of setting the whole thing up and were also sentenced to prison. Of course having cocaine and meth in their new apartment didn't help their case at all.

Chapter 21

Maximum Security Prison

What image does "maximum security prison" bring to mind? Have you ever given any thought as to what it must be like?

Many people never thought they would be working in that kind of environment unless it was a professional decision from the outset of their careers.

I never planned to become an ordained minister any more than I planned to be a Senior Health Educator or Grief and Bereavement Counselor. It was a career that chose me more than I chose it. I have no regrets but I want to share my experiences with anyone who may find him or herself in this situation.

Take a minute and consider what life would be like if you were in a maximum security prison. How you got there is not as important as how you would survive there either as an inmate or grief counselor.

The best accessible example of a maximum security prison is to be found in the movie "The Shawshank Redemption". The prison in that movie has an exercise yard, stone/concrete walls, watch/gun towers with armed guards, row after row of barbed razor wire and fencing, security gates, and a heavy repressed feeling of isolation that can cause a chill to run down anyone's spine.

For the first time in my life I felt the absence of life. I didn't feel as if I was surrounded by death, but I didn't have the feeling of being alive either. It was a very uncomfortable feeling like that of an empty void.

I had never experienced such a feeling before. I have felt fear but never had I the sensation of true evil until my first visit to a maximum security prison.

No matter what your beliefs about good or evil, and whether or not a person can or should be rehabilitated, you cannot make an honest evaluation except from within the walls of this type of prison.

I'm not trying to scare you! But I had to admit to myself I was scared on many levels of consciousness and in conflict with my own beliefs of good vs. evil.

Let us get back to Seth's story. Due to my countless prison visits over the years I always felt "safe" on my visits. I'm not going to say that I never considered what I might do if there were a riot or lock down.

During one visit I did experience a lock down; not because of problems within the prison but because a tornado warning had been issued. No one was permitted to enter or leave the prison until the threatening weather passed. I then truly understood the feeling of losing my freedom.

Yes, it was for my own safety but my insecurity came rushing to the surface and I had to laugh at myself for breaking out in a sweat and feeling a little claustrophobic. I never thought I would have such an experience.

It just goes to prove that life has a way of undermining everything you trust and throws you into total turmoil. As a guard once told me; "Always trust your instincts. If it doesn't feel right get out. Always keep your back to a wall and keep your eyes always moving!" How is that for getting you to relax in a situation?

My first visit with Seth wasn't much different than any of my prior visits to other prisons except for an uneasy feeling. I don't know how to explain it other than it was a feeling you get when you know someone is watching you.

When Seth and I were talking through the bars on my first visit, I noticed his eyes rarely made contact with mine for more than a second or two. I asked him what was going on and he simply stated that he was watching the other inmates just in case something did happen he could take care of himself.

Because of the security level Seth and I were not permitted a contact visit (in a room without bars) so we had to talk on the phone and look at each other through bars on the window. Other inmates would sit in cubicles on either side and this seemed to make every-one nervous.

This is when I first realized I was in an environment of extremely vi-olent people. There were men in this facility who would not hesitate to take another human's life.

Due to distance and travel time I wasn't able to visit Seth as much as I would have liked. No matter how good your intentions, life doesn't always spare you the time or finances to meet your obliga-tions. Most of our communication was by phone or mail and even that was getting expensive.

It didn't take long before I realized I had become Seth's errand boy. He would call me collect and then I would in turn call his family members and let them know how he was doing.

Then he started to request money for envelopes, stamps, writing pa-per, drinks and snacks. I tried to explain to him no matter how much I wanted to help I was having financial difficulties myself and could not afford to supply him with things he needed.

I was really surprised when I started getting collect calls from other inmates I didn't even know and realized it was time to stop all con-tact with Seth.

This didn't set well with Seth but it came to the point where I had to put a block on all prison collect calls and stopped responding to his letters. I didn't like the idea he had given out my personal informa-tion to other inmates in exchange for cigarettes and snacks.

When his family stopped hearing from me they started calling to find out why I had stopped all communication and were not happy about my decision either. I politely informed them he was a member of their family and I was simply a friend. Therefore I suggested they step up as his family and take over all the things I was trying to do to help out. Needless to say I never heard from any of them again.

So here was a very important lesson in working with inmates. You have to become very careful in what you agree to do to help them out. Understand there is a multitude of users and conmen in the prison environment and it is easy for someone on the outside to be set up for use and abuse.

After completing his sentence Seth was released from prison and I was surprised to find him at my front door. I admit I was reluctant to open the door but I had to find out what he wanted.

He had stopped by to apologize for what had taken place during his last incarceration and said he was truly sorry for the way he had treated our friendship and asked for my forgiveness and could we ever be friends again?

I told him I could accept his apology but it would take time to rebuild my trust in him and our friendship. I could come to terms with his reasons for doing what he did but that still didn't mean I trusted him as I had done before. I received a couple of calls from him over the years but now I don't hear anything at all which is probably for the best.

So remember, if you find yourself involved with an inmate be sure to establish your boundaries at the beginning of the relationship. And no matter how much you want to help, keep to those boundaries to prevent becoming a victim of your own dedication to another human being.

Chapter 22

Maximum Security Summary

Let's review by seeing how many of the following questions you can answer. Base your answers on what you feel and think about bereavement with the incarcerated.

1. Based on this story, how many of the general grief symptoms could you apply to your own emotions?

2. Can you identify any grief types listed as they might apply to you if you were the visitor in this story?

3. What stages of grief would take place?

4. How many of the myths do you think you might experience?

5. Put yourself in my place and ask yourself what steps would you have taken to take care of yourself?

6. Do you think you could work with this level of grief and bereavement?

Again there are no wrong answers but I want to give you the opportunity to think about how you might have reacted in this situation.

Section Four

Grief and Bereavement on Death Row

Chapter 23

Working with Death

This chapter is the reason I wrote this book. I never thought I would work on death row, and in retrospect, I wasn't fully prepared for the experience.

I have been at the bedside of too many individuals who succumbed to AIDS starting around 1984. It was because of my volunteer work over the years that I was asked to become a minister. Admittedly it took about a year before I made up my mind and I agreed to be ordained in 1995.

After my ordination, my work with death and dying issues increased and I learned to deal with deaths not just from AIDS but also resulting from suicide, accidents, cancer, heart attacks, overdoses, and the legal right to disconnect life support, so being with someone at the time of death was nothing new for me.

I have witnessed people pass away peacefully for whom death was a relief from their suffering. I was once asked if I thought it was a sin to pray for someone to die and I replied, "Yes, I do believe it is a sin to pray for someone's death, but I did not believe it was a sin to pray to God to end one's suffering!"

Many might disagree with this statement but if you have never dealt with a loved one's long- term suffering you don't have the right to pass judgment on those who have.

Desiring to end a loved one's suffering can put a burden of guilt on a survivor. No one has the right to judge or condemn a person's desire to see the end for the one they love most in life.

If you have never sat at the bed side of one you love and told them it was OK to let go, that you loved them enough to let them go, then I have to question whether you are prepared to do just that and when the time comes will you be able to let them go?

Death is the only guarantee we have in life. It is inevitable; none of us can avoid it, and it is the one common denominator. Everything in between the time we are born to the time we die is called living and we need to approach death not as a loss of the loved one but a celebration of the life that person led. It is very difficult to do but very necessary.

My mother fought COPD (chronic obstructive pulmonary disease) for approximately eighteen years of which the final two years included degenerative spine disease.

Over those years we lost her nearly five times. Each time she came back to us she stated it was so much easier going to the other side than coming back and each time she questioned why she had to come back.

For my family it was getting very difficult and emotionally draining. Each time we thought we were going to lose her each of us went through our typical grief and bereavement process only to have her return to us yet again.

It wasn't that we didn't cherish the additional time we had with her, but it was obvious it was   taking a greater toll on her than anyone else.

When the time came she openly stated to each of her children she was ready and wanted to go to be with her family on the other side. We were in agreement it was time to let her go.

We had plenty of opportunities to say our goodbyes and understood the kind of life she loved was no longer possible for her. Her whole life was now spent inside her home and even though we did everything we could for her it was a lonely existence for her. She had buried her youngest child, two husbands, seven brothers and sisters, and her parents. She lived to be 80 years old which is the longest anyone in our family had ever survived and as she stated many times she was tired and wanted to rest.

Loving her as we did the decision was made it was best to just let her go. We had to accept our desire for her to continue to fight resulted from our own fear of losing her.

When she made her final decision to let go we explained she had to convince the doctors of her desire to stop the fight and give in to the natural course of things. We could sense the relief in her attitude and promised her we would assist in making the transition as easy for her as we possibly could.

Above the pain and sorrow, love is understanding and accepting what all of us must face sometime or another. Telling her it was OK to go and verbally confirming our love for her was the best thing we could have done for her. Yes, I still miss her terribly, but I accepted my loss was nothing compared to what she lost in quality of life due to her suffering   The memories I have of her will be with me the rest of my life.

Chapter 24

Preparing for Death Row

I'll never forget the day I received a call asking if I would be the Spiritual Counselor for someone who had been convicted of murder. I was informed in detail as to why he was on death row and he was truly guilty of the crime of which he had been convicted, and he was looking forward to his execution.

I was also asked if I would be willing to witness his execution on behalf of his family so none of them would have to. He had given up his rights to all appeals and was pressuring the state to execute him as swiftly as possible.

With my previous experience I felt capable of taking on this request. I explained it was not going to be solely my choice to be the inmate's spiritual counselor but it had to be a mutual decision between both him and I.

I would be more than willing to meet with him and if we both decided it would be beneficial I would take on the challenge and responsibility of being his spiritual counselor. Little did I know that decision would take up two and a half years of my life.

After exchanging several letters with the inmate we reached a mutual understanding that I would visit with him giving each of us the opportunity to size up the other. After the necessary paper work, with the help of his lawyer, family, and the prison Chaplain our meeting time and date was scheduled.

The drive was going to be a long one but I always looked forward to long drives when visiting inmates since the drive home gave me the opportunity to debrief myself and get my emotions and thoughts under control. Visiting a prison will bring unexpected professional and personal issues to the surface, let alone the issues I would have to face working on death row.

Working with my first death row inmate I knew I would have to look deeply into my own beliefs about the death penalty and what part my religious upbringing would play in such a situation. My spiritual and religious beliefs were always in conflict and I knew this situation would raise many questions I had never considered before.

It never ceases to amaze me how we as humans can have ideas and opinions about issues when we may never have had any experience in working with or around such issues. We tend to believe our own concepts and ideas are always the correct ones and are very hesitant and reluctant to accept a change in the ideas we feel a strong commitment to.

I learned very quickly other ministers of my acquaintance were not so open to hearing my concerns about the best way to help this inmate. Several just simply walked away and some just wished me luck and hoped I would find answers for my questions. It didn't take me long to realize I was getting ready to go on a journey I would be taking mostly by myself.

Over the two and a half years there were individuals who came forth to help me prepare and all of them were working within the system of death row and had experience with executions. It seemed providential they should come at exactly the time I needed them most.

Fortunately I belonged to a group of funeral home directors, Chaplains, Grief and Bereavement Counselors, Grief Educators and so forth. This GriefWork group became more important to me than they would ever know.

They would step in whenever they saw I was getting too involved with the situation and were always open to not only talking with me but most importantly listening to me.

Before our first meeting I had read everything I could on the inmate, his history of stays in jail and prison, the type of crimes he had committed before the murder charge, tried to get as much family background information as I could, all in an attempt to have a basis on whether or not I would, could, or should be his spiritual counselor.

I knew I could very easily become part of the media circus that always surrounds murderers and the death penalty. I didn't want any of this to interfere with the job I was about to take on, and, yes, I did think of it as a job.

I had to be able to put aside the media concept of who they said he was, try my best not to let the inmate's family sway me in any way, or disassociate myself from the victim's family and what they would be going through. I was determined to trust my thoughts and feelings based on how we interacted with each other and not let anyone else be of influence.

I had to develop trust between us by not getting caught up in any games or crisis which was not part of his spiritual salvation. I needed to push aside my own beliefs and emotions about the crime and concentrate strictly on our interaction during visits and then process everything on my way home. For the love of God what was I doing and how did I get to this place in my life?

Did I have doubts? -- Plenty. Was I as confident on the drive up for the first visit as I had been on the phone when I had agreed to do this? -- No way! Could I keep all the promises I had made to myself, the inmate, and his family? I wasn't so sure anymore, but I had made a promise and an obligation and I knew I had to follow through for my own peace of mind.

The inmate and his family told me if it ever got to be too much to simply stop, walk away, and go back to my own life. I was thrilled to know there was a way out, but I've never been one not to complete a job once started.

103

This situation was not going to be any different as far as my dedication was concerned, and I knew I had taken on a responsibility very few individuals would ever have the opportunity to experience.

As a minister, as a counselor, as a human being committed to helping others how could I not take on such an opportunity? I knew it would be life changing. I knew there were going to be challenges I had never had to face before, and my life would be changed forever but more importantly I wanted this challenge.

What challenges would I have to face to prepare myself for the task? I made the following list:

1. Unsavory details about the crime.
2. Family issues surrounding the crime.
3. The victim's family issues about the crime.
4. Barriers to communication.
5. Barriers to intimacy.
6. Barriers to honesty.
7. Barriers to physical contact.
8. Policies of religion of all parties.
9. Time countdown.
10. Logistics.
11. Issues around mental illness.
12. Multiple layers of guilt.
13. Guilt related to the past.
14. Family correlation involving emotional and social dysfunction.
15. Communication issues between me and the inmate.
16. Intimacy issues in my own life.
17. Would I be accepted by the inmate?
18. Would I be accepted by his family?
19. Was I doing the right thing?
20. And of course the most difficult of all, issues dealing with the different perspectives created by the media.

Chapter 25

Death Row – The Beginning

The day I arrived for my first visit I admit I was a little nervous. I'm always nervous the first day I visit a new prison, since I never know exactly how I will be received by the staff and security officers. Since this was my first death row encounter, I had no idea what to expect.

The entrance was no different from the other prisons I had been to so that reassured me a little. I went to the window to check in and the person working the desk had no idea I was on anyone's visitation list. Even though I was in full clergy apparel and obviously there for clerical purposes they didn't seem to give a damn.

Another officer came on duty at the security desk and asked me what I was doing there. When I explained I was on my first visit for an inmate on death row he told me I did not have to report to the window for check in. The window was used only for visitations in the general population.

Since I was established as the spiritual counselor for a death row inmate all of my visits would be pre-cleared through the warden's office and all I had to do was check-in at security.

Once I was checked in and went through the security screening I had to wait to be buzzed for entrance to the holding area. After a few minutes in the holding area I was buzzed through to be escorted to the death row building. I had no idea the death row unit would be totally separated from the main prison and have its own security check-in process.

When I finally arrived at the death row facility, I was buzzed in once again and had to show my hand stamp and paper work. After the security check-in I was escorted to the waiting area while they went to get the prisoner. I'll call this inmate Mitch.

I was under the impression I would have a full contact visit with Mitch and was not happy about spending the next four or five hours sitting on a wooden chair talking through a phone and looking through a piece of bullet proof glass. But then again I am on death row, or so I thought. I was in the death row general visitation area and was not on death row at all.

When they brought Mitch into the visiting area he was in what I will call a five-way shackle system. He was wearing wrist shackles, ankle shackles, and had a chain around his waist that both shackles were attached to. Then the guard padlocked him to the floor once he was in his chair.

To think I was complaining about having to spend the next four or five hours sitting on a wooden chair. Throughout the visit I could see just how uncomfortable Mitch was holding the phone and switching it back and forth.

I don't know what I had expected but was pleasantly surprised to discover that Mitch had a wonderful sense of humor. He seemed to have a mellow type of personality and I had difficulty accepting the fact this man was guilty of murdering another human being.

We would banter back and forth making light of the whole situation and drilling each other to find out where each stood on different issues. This part of our meeting I expected and would have been disappointed if the bantering didn't take place. We didn't discuss any thing about the crime but spent the entire visit getting to know one another.

Toward the end of the visit, we did discuss not having a contact visit and he said he would talk to the prison Chaplin and see what had gone wrong. I on the other hand was going to call the warden's office the next day and double check to insure all the proper paperwork had been submitted. The whole purpose of my being there was to have a contact visit with Mitch so we could discuss privately all of his upcoming issues.

106

Driving home after the visit I took time to stop for lunch and just sat and thought about our meeting and was positive that I would be able to be Mitch's spiritual counselor. Of course the final decision was still up to Mitch, but I had a feeling we had connected and there would be more visits in my future.

Mitch did accept me as his spiritual counselor, but it took two more visits before we were able to get all of the paperwork in order for the contact visit. It's not easy working within a system with departments that don't seem to work well together. (Welcome to bureaucracy!)

I was able to acquire the phone number of an employee in the warden's office who would be my contact for all future visits. All I had to do in future was to call them and schedule my visits.

Once the reservation was made by phone, I still had to submit a letter stating the date and time of my visit so they keep track of all my visits. I didn't mind for the sake of my own convenience.

Since I lived so far away I informed her my visits would always be at 9:00 am and I would stay three to five hours. Over time, many of the guards and employees were stunned a clergyman would visit for such a length of time.

Side note: During one of my visits in the general visiting area another inmate stopped and started talking with Mitch. This inmate was a blue eyed, dark haired, well built, handsome man. The type you see on the cover of exercise, GQ, sports, or any other men's magazines. His smile was bright and his teeth were the type any dentist would be proud to claim as his work.

He asked Mitch to introduce me and tried to start up a conversation. Mitch explained I was his spiritual counselor and would help to prepare him for his execution. Then the inmate asked if I would be willing to be his spiritual counselor once Mitch was gone.

What happened next stunned me. He started fondling himself and was starting to become sexually aroused. Apparently the guards noticed it too and removed him from the area immediately.

Once he was out of hearing range, I asked Mitch what that was all about and Mitch told me he was a serial killer and used his looks to seduce young men and women. Once he got them home he would torture and sexually abuse them before cutting their throats. Once they were dead he would sexually assault them again.

Unbelievable to think how easily his looks and his charm must have made it for him to lure his victims. My discomfort was turning into fear and disgust that one human could not only think of such horrific crimes but also commit them.

I asked Mitch if he knew how many victims the man had killed and Mitch said rumors put it at around eight to ten known victims. The authorities really didn't know how many there were but were certain there were more victims than he was admitting to.

Whatever concepts I had about working on death row were all in question. The reality of where I was came crashing down hard. From that moment on I had difficulty in speaking with Mitch and remaining friendly while always holding onto the idea he was a murderer as well.

My life had taken me to a place many people and professionals would never want to go, but here I was in one of the smallest and darkest corners of existence. Everything I had ever believed, I was questioning. For the first time in my life I realize there are individuals among us who are evil and I have no doubt that many of them are beyond rehabilitation.

Midway through my drive home I pulled into a rest area and just sat at one of the picnic tables and gave some serious thought to what I was doing. Mr. Blue Eyes had unexpectedly destroyed all of my confidence.

108

It's difficult to explain with words just what it was like to look into the eyes of a serial killer. The intense feeling of a deceptively deep dark evil was hiding behind the eyes of this killer. A deep chill along your spine which triggers all of your defenses.

I must have sat there for over an hour before I felt I was ready to continue my drive. I didn't want to take this dirty evil feeling into my home so I had to pull it together. I know my clothes weren't dirty but I felt my spirit had been soiled to the very core and there is no way to wash that feeling away.

If I was going to work with Mitch I knew I had to get over these sensations. If I couldn't learn to control these fears, I would appear weak to the death row inmates and that was the last thing I wanted. I had to be more confident than I had ever been in my whole life if I was going to pull this off. I was determined nothing was going to prevent the fulfillment of this obligation

Chapter 26

Death Row Contact Visit

We finally succeeded in arranging and scheduling our first contact visit. I'm ready and looking forward to visiting Mitch and not worrying about visits from other inmates. I wanted to be able to give Mitch my complete attention and to have as few interruptions as possible. I had made a commitment and I wanted to follow through with it to the best of my ability.

I assumed by now there would be no more surprises and I really wasn't looking forward to any but there were more in store for me. It started with my arrival at the prison for our contact visit and didn't end until I got home that evening.

I signed in at the main desk, went through the security screening, received my visitor ID, cleared through the first metal door, waited, cleared through the second metal door then waited for my security escort.

I was informed the contact visit would take place INSIDE death row and not at the general visiting area. I had to pass through four more electronically controlled gates just to get to death row housing.

Next I had to be buzzed into the building, show my ID, scan my hand stamp, buzzed through one of the biggest, heaviest, metal doors I have ever seen outside of a bank vault.

Once on the other side of the door I was greeted by another security officer and escorted below ground and through a long tunnel to another huge metal door. The door was buzzed open and I had to sign in and wait for another prison guard escort.

The officer escorted me through four more gates made of heavy metal bars. These gates all had different keys for operation and when I arrived at death row there was another heavy duty door through which I had to be buzzed in. Once inside, I signed in at the security area and was told to take a seat and wait.

This room had bullet proof windows that looked onto the death row inmate's living area. Each cell was a one-man-cell and located on two levels. Fencing and gates separated the two levels right down the middle. One or two inmates at a time were permitted out of their cells but were limited as to where they could go or who they could talk to.

As I was signing in, who do you think was the first inmate I saw on the other side of the glass?

If you guessed the blue-eyed monster you would be right. While I had my head down signing in, I asked the guard if I should ignore him, flip him off, or throw him a kiss. The guard got a chuckle out of this and responded it would make his day to see a minister flip off an inmate but the best thing to really piss off this particular inmate was to ignore him completely and so I did.

After about 20 minutes of talking with the guards one of them escorted me into a room with a couple of chairs, a table, and one of the biggest eyebolts I had ever seen imbedded in a concrete floor under the table. This would be where the inmate would be chained to the floor throughout the visit.

I was instructed to sit in a chair and push it all the way up against the wall. If the inmate started to act up, I was to get out of the door as fast as possible and they would handle the situation. I asked if this happened often with Mitch and they said they didn't know what if anything he would do since this was his first contact visit.

So there I was sitting in a room in the middle of death row housing with nothing to protect me except the five guards who were on duty. If anything did happen I had no idea how to get out, or the worst feeling of all, would I be able to.get out. I may not have been sentenced here, but I was as locked down as the guards and inmates. In other words, my life was definitely in God's hands and all I could do was pray everything would go smoothly.

Mitch was escorted into the room with one of the biggest smiles I could have hoped for. He was joking with the guards as they chained his shackles to the floor, pulled his chair up to the table and said, and I quote: "Well preacher man welcome to my world! I'm glad you're here but I have to admit I didn't think you had the balls to come all the way back here to death row."

My response was simply, "Dude, you have no idea how big my balls are and I'll show them to you if you want to avoid making any more bad judgments!" Not a comment you would expect from a minister but he laughed, the guards laughed, and so started a relationship built on one liners, humor, bickering, and an easy feeling we would be able to work well together.

The conversation started off slowly with discussions about my drive up and did I have any hassles with getting back to death row.

We spent several hours talking about his family and how they were holding up threw all of this and what ideas if any did I have which could make life a little easier for them. We explored the concepts of spirituality vs. religion, what he was seeking from me as his spiritual counselor, did he really want to learn and seek salvation, or just use me as a visitation break.

For the first time he was opening up about his childhood and family life which was very important for me to hear and understand. Without that information, there was no way I could comprehend what led up to his murdering someone, giving up his right to appeal, and trying to rush his execution.

We ended the visit after four hours, and both of us were on good terms about how the visit had turned out. As soon as I was able to confirm the next visit I would let him know and give him something to look forward to. Admittedly I was looking forward to our next visit as well.

A lot of time and energy had gone into getting to this point and as I look back it was well worth it. I was going to face challenges I had never dreamed of and I now accepted the fact I could and would face these challenges.

That evening I called some of his family and let them know how he was doing, how the visit had played out, his acceptance of me as his spiritual counselor, and my personal commitment that I would be able to do what was being asked of me.

Over the next two and a half years I used the time between visits to analyze what I wanted to achieve in the next visit. Where the conversations would end up was up to Mitch, but I tried to have a basic list of issues to cover and information requested by his family.

He was very inquisitive about different types of spirituality and I suggested books he could get from the prison library on Native American, Celtic, Nordic, Pagan, and Wicca religious beliefs as well as those of Buddhism, Catholicism, Judaism, and Protestantism. I suggested studying different types of meditation, stress management, and relaxation.

During one of our visits he admitted he was raised Christian but feared due to his crime he could not be a Christian in good standing again. After many months of conversation and exploration of other cultures and religions Mitch was becoming more open to returning to his Christian beliefs. According to his therapist this was a major step for Mitch and all the research was helping him pass the time productively instead of just sitting in his cell waiting.

When the weather permitted, the guards would put Mitch out in the small exercise area and I could sit on the outside of the fence. We were permitted to smoke whenever he was in the exercise area and the visits became more and more like two buddies hanging out in the back yard.

I always tried to let Mitch lead the conversation and when he was in high spirits the visits were always comical. As I said before, he had

114

a wonderful sense of humor, as do I, and it would turn into a joke fest. Looking back now I have to

admit I miss those visits. It made me feel good knowing I could bring a little bit of happiness into such a dismal place.

When Mitch's mood was low the visits were a little bit more complicated. His anger towards the guards, his therapist, lawyer, governor, law makers, media, and sometimes different family members made it difficult to keep him on track. We never did get into a screaming match but we came very close several times.

When our personalities were in conflict, I simply left the room and went out to the guard's area and sat down. This was a signal to both the guards and Mitch that I needed to calm myself and figure out a completely new approach.

I'm happy to say there was only one time over those years when Mitch just was not in control of his anger. It was the only time I ever threatened to walk out of a visit and not come back. I maintained my composure and calmly told him I didn't drive all the way up there to spend three or four hours listening to him complain and act like a spoiled four year old.

Needless to say he didn't like what I had said and for the first time we were at the point of seeing who was going to back down first. I could see it in his eyes, he wanted to blow up and read me the riot act. He could see in my eyes I was not going to put up with it, and as cruel as it might be to say, I had the advantage of walking out if I chose.

This was going to be a breaking point in our relationship. A point I had hoped we would never come to but now that we were I couldn't back down no matter what the outcome might be. It was time to lay all the cards on the table and call his bluff.

I told him to think before he said another word and I was going out of the room to let him think about what he was going to say when I came back in. I wanted him to see I was not then nor was I ever going to be his whipping post. His words would determine whether I would be in his future.

Sitting out with the guards they knew this was a major test for Mitch and fortunately did not intervene. They had developed a respect for what I was trying to do with Mitch and knew it was going to be a major judgment call on his part.

While out there with the guards they quietly let me know they hoped I could call his bluff. Since I had been working with Mitch they had seen a major change in his attitude and he was as a result a much better inmate. They claimed they had gotten to the point of enjoying his company when he was out of his cell and his relationship with the other inmates was calmer and non-threatening.

After about twenty or thirty minutes one of the guards went to check how Mitch was doing. The first thing Mitch asked the guard was if I was sitting out there waiting for him to calm down. When the guard told him I was he asked him to ask me to come back in so we could talk. A major step since he had requested, not ordered me, to come back in.

As soon as I was back in the room he wanted to know if we could "kiss and make up". I told him I didn't have a problem with making up but I wasn't too fond of the kissing part. "You're just not my type!" Mitch, the guard, and I exploded with laughter and I knew all was well for now.

Chapter 27

Death Penalty Crime

I never questioned Mitch about the crime that put him on death row. I knew all about it from the media and his family, but I hadn't heard his story of what had happened.

I intended to work my question into some of our conversations but I didn't feel right about bringing up the subject. I decided the best approach would be to let him tell me when he felt it would be beneficial for him to share the story.

I'd been working with Mitch for a little under a year and the subject of the crime never entered the conversation until now. It was a typical spring with about sixteen days of overcast gray skies, on and off rain, and the kind of weather that can put anyone in a deep-blue funk.

It was on one of those gray days that Mitch decided to share his story of the crime. After all this time of waiting to hear that story I was not prepared for the graphic details he was about to describe but there was no backing out now. As they say "be careful of what you wish for" and this was definitely one of those times.

The visit started with our usual catching up. We talked about his family, what was going on with his lawyer and the courts over his refusing to do any appeals, why he had filed a petition to withdraw his not guilty plea, waived his rights to a jury trial, and why he wanted to rush his execution.

I don't know if I will be able to convey fully what I saw, felt, and heard. I've always believed any human being could be rehabilitated. I was not prepared to learn this isn't always the case and what a lesson it turned out to be.

As I stated earlier Mitch had a history of trouble with the law. As a teenager he had been sent to a school for the behaviorally handicapped and emotionally disturbed children. There seemed to be evidence of sexual abuse in and outside the home which lead Mitch to becoming sexually abusive with other children.

Mitch had been involved with petty crimes at a very early age. He served a seven year prison term and was released in the late 1990's. As with many long term inmates he had a great deal of trouble adapting to the outside world and turned his focus on getting back into prison.

After trying to survive in the outside world, he committed another burglary which put him back in prison where he wanted to be. He was sentenced to serve eight years for having a weapon under disability (he was classified as mentally disabled), attempted burglary and attempted escape.

I'm not going to go into every detail of what Mitch did to his victim out of respect for the family of the victim and Mitch's. Both families had been through enough. However, I have to emphasize that he did not merely commit a murder but butchered and slaughtered another human being.

As Mitch was telling me of this horrid crime and slipped deeper into the details of what he had done, I witnessed something come over him I had never seen before. It was the complete transformation of a man whose company I had come to enjoy into a man of pure violence who had obviously delighted in what he had done.

The look in his eyes changed from friendly and happy to dark and menacing. His voice changed as he became more emotionally excited telling me the story of his murderous act. He took me on a journey into the deepest darkest valleys of human treachery and evil.

After his story we both sat in silence and I observed him coming out of a trance-like state. After a couple of minutes back in reality he apologized and said he never intended to go into as much detail about how and why he had committed the crime.

His first concern was if I was OK and would I continue my visits. I lied and said I was fine when of course I was not. I stated I didn't enjoy listening to his story but I knew what I was getting into when I accepted the offer to be his spiritual counselor.

To my surprise I found myself asking if he would kill again if he ever got out. For the first time he admitted to being a pedophile and stated he would kill again. I followed up with the question of why he felt he *would* kill again and his response was simple and again I quote: "Dan, once you cross the unwritten line of taking another man's life you experience a rush like no other on the planet." "Once you've experienced such a rush the only way to duplicate it is to kill again and again!"

"To break one of the most moral laws of the universe is a one way ticket from which you can never go back." "My next victim if they ever released me would be someone's child and I don't want that to happen, so execute me now!" These were his words and I have no doubt they were true.

The rest of the visit was uneventful to say the least and I was able to maintain my focus and keep the turmoil I was experiencing under control. I couldn't let him sense how his story had affected me and I was determined I would stay cool, calm, and reserved until my drive home.

The drive home was the most unnerving experience I had ever had. There weren't enough rest areas where my emotions could run their course. Every time I thought I was OK I'd get back on the highway and then have another emotional episode.

I had just sat with a man who enjoyed taking another man's life! The details of the crime were like being in a horror movie but I was sitting there across the table from the man who had committed the crime.

I question everything I believed in morally and ethically. I thought about quitting but was too involved to back out now. I couldn't tell his family I didn't want to represent him anymore without telling them his story and I didn't want to repeat that nightmare at all!

By the time I reached the last rest area before home I pulled over and sat at one of the picnic tables for over two hours. I had to let all my emotions run their course. I felt nauseous, flushed, and unsure I could handle anymore.

I realized the only way I could handle all of this was to permit myself to relive every bit of the story. It was like a bad accident on the highway where you can't keep yourself from looking even though you know you will regret it.

It would be unhealthy for me to repress anything I was feeling, and like it or not, I had to face every detail and use it as a learning tool. Analyze the emotion, accept it, and move on to the next emotion and repeat the process until I was exhausted and able to come to terms with what I had just experienced.

By the time I got home, I felt I could resume my life and look forward to what I had to be thankful for. My only concern now was whether I could go to sleep that night without having any nightmares. Fortunately, I was so exhausted I didn't go to sleep; I simply passed out and I am still thankful for a dreamless night's rest.

Chapter 28

Date of Execution

After the fateful visit with Mitch, everything settled into a routine of meetings with his lawyer, meetings with the state Religious Services Administrator (RSA), meetings with the family, and visits with Mitch.

Throughout all of his court appearances, Mitch continued to press for his own execution. He told me many times he preferred to be executed than spend the rest of his life in total isolation. Mitch explained it to me this way: "The cost for them to keep me locked up for one year would be enough to pay for two teachers' salaries and I would rather see two teachers employed than me spending my life in here!"

Now the stage had been set and so had the execution date. Everything took on a different perspective as everyone focused on the upcoming execution. For all the families it was taking time off from their jobs, booking hotel rooms, making travel arrangements, and preparing to say their final goodbyes.

For me it was working with Mitch to prepare him for his impending death. What could I do for him in those last weeks? Was he prepared for his inevitable death?

To my surprise, Mitch asked if I felt comfortable enough to baptize him. He wanted to be baptized as a Christian and do whatever he could to make peace between himself and God. I explained I could make arrangements for him to be baptized but I could not be the one to do the baptism.

I could not bring the things necessary for baptism into the prison; therefore the state Religious Services Administrator would be the one who would do the baptism. Mitch accepted this and I started making all the necessary arrangements.

I had several phone calls with the RSA about how we felt about Mitch's request for baptism. By this time, we didn't know if this was another con or if he really did want to be baptized. We concluded that it was not our place to question Mitch's request but our obligation as ministers to fulfill it.

There has always been controversy over a convicted murderer asking for baptism and receiving religious salvation. My response to this is it is not a minister's place to pass judgment but his/her obligation to fulfill the request for spiritual or religious forgiveness and salvation. It is up to the good Lord to make the final decision about salvation with those who have committed murder.

I knew my position was to assist Mitch in every detail of his death and the list of questions went something like this:

1. What did he want done with his personal belongings?

2. Was he writing his goodbye letters to his family members?

3. Did he want to be buried or cremated and who would be responsible for paying for it?

4. If he did choose cremation what did he want done with his ashes?

5. Did he want a funeral service for the benefit of his family?

6. Did he want me to witness the execution on behalf of his family or were there family members who could be witnesses?

7. Was he preparing his final press release and statement?

8. Whom did he want or not want to visit him on his last day?

9. Had he made his request for his last meal?

10. Was there anyone outside of his family for me to contact?

11. What were his final wishes?

12. What was left that I could do for him?

As they say; "so many questions, so much to do, and so little time!" I had made it this far on the journey and I needed to make sure I could complete it to the best of my ability.

As time raced by everything seemed to be falling into place and everyone involved was on pins and needles. The reality of what was about to happen had sunk in and the question on everyone's mind was "Is this it? Is this really going to happen?"

I was getting very frustrated with not being able to find any materials which could help with what I, my client, and the client's family was preparing for. There were books on working through grief with the death of a pet, suicide, loss of a parent or loss of a child, and so forth and so on.

That was when I realized once this was all over, with the permission of Mitch and his family; I needed to write a book to assist other clergy, social workers, counselors, or family members who would find themselves in this exact situation.

It's not every day you work with someone who knows the exact date, time, and method of his death. Everything I knew about grief had to be applied in reverse. That's when I realized the grieving process started back in the court room when the prisoner was found guilty and sentenced. Once the execution took place all the "normal" grieving processes would then be put into action for all of the survivors.

Thanks to all the members of GriefWorks I found a treasure trove of support, suggestions, and concerns for my own well being. This group was made up of grief and bereavement counselors, funeral home directors, social workers, clergy, and other professionals in the field. It was with their support I was able to find the tools I needed to make it through the execution process.

Everything was in place and everyone was as prepared as they could be for the execution. Then just as time seemed to speed up it just as suddenly began to slow down. Time seemed to be crawling by and conversations became difficult after all of the goodbyes had been said.

Mitch and I had a little difficulty in finding things to discuss or laugh about during my visits. Once we knew death was knocking at the door what was left to talk about that seemed to have any importance?

Each visit now became more of a checklist of what we had gone over many times and even though we knew there was nothing left to check off of the list we reviewed it again and again just to be sure. We needed to confirm that nothing and no one was left unattended. Mitch wanted everything to go as smoothly and painlessly as possible for his family.

Chapter 29

Execution Postponed

Everybody is on the same page and preparing for the execution. The family members have made their travel plans and reservations, Mitch is counting down the hours, the prison has made all of the arrangements necessary for transportation to the death house as they called it, his lawyer had all of the press releases ready, and I'm working the best I can with being in the middle of everything.

My visitations with Mitch were nothing more than attempts to keep his spirits high and focused on what was about to happen. I was always questioning him about any last minute wishes or problems. It seemed unbelievable that the time was so near after a little over two years of working with Mitch.

Then we received the call no one expected. The Governor granted a reprieve so he could review the case and all the records. I could understand him not wanting to rush into an execution but I can't accept he was unaware of the trauma he was going to cause everyone. Everyone was ready for closure and now they wouldn't be able to have the closure they had been so nervously waiting for.

When I received the call from Mitch's lawyer we agreed he would contact Mitch and I would contact the family members. This meant all reservations, travel plans, vacation time and grieving would have to be readjusted and put on hold.

For Mitch's family, the hardest part of their grieving process would come by dealing with the anger of the postponement followed by the guilt of wanting the whole thing to be over, and the anger, fear, remorse, and frustration of being thrown back into an unknown situation.

Everyone was prepared to say their farewells and anxious to bring an end to the drama. Now all anyone could do was wait and see if the Governor would approve the execution or change Mitch's sentence to life in prison without parole.

Family members may often want an execution over a life-sentence so that they can return to a normal life. This can cause major guilt and hurt feelings within the family. A life sentence for an inmate means a life sentence of too few visits, social ridicule, family arguments, and heartache.

On the other hand they loved Mitch and didn't want him to die. He was loved by his family and here was the possibility of keeping Mitch alive. This in itself would cause intense guilt because the family knew Mitch didn't want to spend the rest of his life on death row and be more of a burden on his family for the next thirty or forty years. It had become a Catch-22 of praying he remained alive against his wishes or praying for his execution and a return to a normal life.

Needless to say, when Mitch found this out he was furious. He was prepared to die and now didn't know what the future held for him. He was ready and willing and felt betrayed by the system. He was overwhelmed with questions about his future.

He was in his early thirties and refused to accept spending another thirty or forty years in lockup. If his wish to be executed was refused he threatened to kill again at his first opportunity. I believed he was desperate to end his life and more than willing to take another life to do so.

The hardest part for his lawyer and I was to get everyone to calm down and accept there was nothing anyone could do. Everything was out of our control and until the Governor made his decision all we could do was play the waiting game and it would not be an easy wait. Everyone involved could do nothing more at that point than wait and pray for the best.

In the days leading up to his execution, Mitch requested little recreation time and to be left alone. He more or less isolated himself in order to help him achieve peace of mind. With his new found Christianity he was spending most of his time reading the Bible, playing chess, or reading magazines. I personally believed it was the first time Mitch had found peace and solitude within himself.

When Mitch and I spoke of his new found Christianity I used it as an opportunity to have Mitch accept this delay as a test of his new commitment. I was sure the Governor would approve the execution and he was doing nothing more than covering his political butt. It was not revenge against Mitch, his family, or anything else other than politics.

He admitted waiting was becoming very difficult and he didn't know if he would be able to wait for the Governor's decision. This set off alarm bells and I told the guards he needed to be on a suicide watch and the waiting was wearing him down spiritually and emotionally.

The guards informed me whenever there is a reprieve so close to the execution date the inmate is put on a suicide watch immediately. They appreciated my concern and apologized for not keeping me up-to-date with prison procedures and promised to keep me better informed of prison policies.

The new execution date had been set but until we heard from the Governor no one knew if the execution would really take place or not. The family was informed of the new date and told to make new reservations but to guarantee they could get their money back in case of another possible delay or change in Mitch's status.

Three months may not seem like a long time but think what your life would be like if you knew there was a good chance you would not be alive in three months.

Think of the strain this would put on you, your family, and loved ones. Knowing you would not be here in three months and having to make a decision on whether to pray for a cure or to pray for a painless demise. It is a heavy burden indeed and this is where the crisscrossing of emotions really takes its toll.

The trauma of anticipatory death is difficult on its own but unfortunately only one of the levels of grief one will experience. There are no clear cut rules on what emotions will surface, or in what order, or time they will appear. The best that any of us can do in such situations is to seek help whenever possible. Accept and believe everything can and will go back to normal.

Chapter 30

One Day Remaining

Things were finally starting to settle down into a routine. Mitch's correspondence with his family had been extremely helpful for him and his family. Our visitations were less depressing than before with little anger and everybody was simply trying to pass the time while quietly waiting for word from the Governor.

Two months had past when I received the call from the lawyer stating the Governor had accepted Mitch's guilty plea and the execution was back on and scheduled to be carried out within the month.

Suddenly everything had kicked into high gear and all involved were back on an emotional roller coaster of confirming all travel plans, hotel reservations, family meetings and visitations.

With the confirmation of his execution my responsibility was to work with Mitch. There were a lot of things we had to get confirmed, signed, and notarized. I would be taking care of his final wishes and distributing his personal belongings and remains. All of our work together was coming to a hard-fought end; however, talking about the end and having confirmation are two separate issues.

I had him write up a list of who was going to get what from his personal belongings and confirmed he had written all of his goodbye letters and cards.

He decided to have his remains cremated and I agreed to divide his ashes among his family members. I asked if he had a specific request for part of his ashes he would want me to carry out. As I promised him I will not share what his specific request was but I am proud to say I was able to keep my obligation in disposing part of his ashes per his request.

He did not want a funeral service but for the benefit of his family I convinced him they needed a service for closure and he agreed to honor their need.

He and his lawyer had taken care of all of his final statements and press releases so I didn't have to concern myself with those issues. We discussed who would or would not be on his visitation list at the death house (the building where the execution would take place) and made all of the appropriate contacts and arrangements.

He had submitted his request for his last meal and it was impressive. As he put it "why worry about calories now? I'm going to enjoy each and every bite and eat a whole chocolate cake!" "I'm in pig heaven!"

Everything was in proper order, confirmed, recorded and awaiting his execution. My last visit before his transfer to the death house was one of mixed emotions. The conversation between Mitch and I was one of the most sincere conversations we had had over the last two and a half years.

I assume the confirmation of death overrides any and all game playing. I honestly believed everything about our conversation was from his heart and in gratitude for the work we had accomplished.

I was confused by my own emotions at the time because I knew a murderer was going to be executed but I was overcome by sadness as though I was losing a friend. I had tried to maintain a professional relationship and distance between Mitch and I but with all we had shared over the years it was more difficult than I had anticipated.

Right or wrong, professional or not, I was going to miss Mitch. He had become an intricate part of my professional life and I realized I was going to have to face my own grief which was something that had not occurred to me. I could never have done or accomplished what I had if I hadn't built some sort of a personal relationship with Mitch. How can one be spiritual and not make a human connection?

The drive to my hotel the day before the execution fortunately was a sunny beautiful day. I admit I cheated and took the longest route possible simply to enjoy the weather and time alone. I had plenty of time to get there and I wanted to experience and enjoy as much of my surroundings as I could.

The last thing Mitch had asked me before his transfer to the death house was to sway the prison to let him out of death row so he could lie in the grass under a shade tree. Since he was marked for execution the prison refused his last wish due to security reasons and he had to spend his remaining time surrounded by the same concrete and metal bars he had been living with over the past years.

It sounded like a simple request but it was not going to happen at the prison or at the death house. I admit it perturbed me to think I could not fulfill such a simple request for a man scheduled to die within a couple of days. Many might say he did not deserve special treatment but just how special was it to want to lie in the grass and feel the warmth of sunshine?

This was why I took the long drive and stopped along the way to lie in the grass, under a big shade tree, and feel the warmth of the sun. I couldn't get it for Mitch but I realized just how important it was for me to do it for myself.

After arriving at the hotel I met with the lawyer and the state Religious Services Administrator. They voiced their concerns on whether or not I was prepared for what was about to happen. I answered their questions and explained to them yes this was my first execution but not the first time I had dealt with death. I had been at death's bedside many times before and had been in a position of giving the order to disconnect someone's life support against family wishes.

Mitch's execution was going to be by lethal injection and I knew I would be able to cope with witnessing the procedure. If his execution would have been by electric chair, firing squad, or hanging I could not and would not have been a witness. And yes all of the forms of execution are still legal in some states.

My major concerns were being able to meet all of Mitch's needs and then shift my attention to the needs of his family after the execution. I was with his family members when they arrived at the death house visitor's holding area and the next day escorted one relative for visitation on his last day.

I met most of his family before his transfer to the death house, but the reality of the situation was still in limbo and the emotional feelings were not as heavy as they were now or going to be after confirmation of his execution.

So there we were sitting in the holding area as the family members were each waiting their turns to visit. Only two family members at a time could visit Mitch in the death house. Mitch was shackled to the floor of the room but family members did have the opportunity to hug him goodbye. With one exception, this would be the last time his relatives would see Mitch alive. After their respective visits they all agreed to return to the hotel.

I promised Mitch I would stay and be available by request if he needed me. Once the family had left he did summon me for some last minute details he wanted carried out.

During all of these visitations there was what is called the "Death Team Members". No less than six guards were observing and recording everything said, the movement of personnel, the inmate, visitors in and out of the death house and time was recorded approximately every 5 minutes.

The death team members started arriving at 8:30 in the morning to prepare for Mitch's arrival and remained until the execution process was complete and they were relieved of their duties. Over a day and a half of watching, recording, and listening because the state did not want to risk any possible errors.

132

Chapter 31

Execution

Needless to say I didn't sleep well the night before his execution and I had to be up bright and early for a meeting at the Death House. I was asked to meet with the prison minister and the lawyer to go over the final details and procedures for the day.

We were now in the final hours of Mitch's life and I was preparing for my first visit with Mitch where I would be given all of his personal belongings which, at his request, I would distributed to his family at a later date.

My next visit was with a relative whom I had escorted to and from the Death House. I helped prepare her for the visit by informing her that the visit would take place at the death house and not in the same visiting area where she had been the day before.

I wanted her to understand the only contact she would have would be holding hands through the bars and the Death Team would be watching every move and recording the visit. Mitch and I had tried to talk her out of this visit but she was persistent and Mitch finally gave in to her request.

After our visit this relative left the prison. It was a difficult visitation for both Mitch and this member of his family but Mitch seemed to be happy they had had the opportunity to say goodbye.

My job now was one of sitting and waiting. The mental health team had to do their evaluation, the medical team had to be cleared for entry to the death house and all of their preparations completed. The funeral director had arrived and the Warden was on site.

First the victim's witnesses were called to the death house viewing room then the inmate's witnesses were called to the same area. Last but not least selected media personnel were escorted into the viewing area and waited with the rest of us.

Once they were ready to proceed, they opened the curtains to the death room and there in the middle was the execution table that reminded me of a horizontal crucifix. The cross was an instrument of execution and it seemed so ironic it was still being used in modern society today.

Everyone sat in silence while Mitch was escorted into the execution room and lay on the table. He had a smile on his face and was joking with the Warden. Once he was restrained the prison minister prayed with him and Mitch made a statement of apology to the victim's family.

Once the drugs were administered it didn't take long before all was over for Mitch. I had been with people when they died but observing an execution was a totally different experience to say the least.

I couldn't feel sorry for Mitch since I had been with people who had died a more horrendous death than what I just witnessed. Mitch died by his own hands and by his own request. His death appeared to be one of a peaceful crossing and I could only hope when my time came I would go as easily as he seemed to.

I left the prison and returned to the hotel looking forward to some quiet time to be alone and to contemplate what I had just experienced. I would be having dinner with the lawyer and prison minister later in the evening but what I wanted at that moment was to stand in the shower and let the steaming hot water relax every tired muscle in my body.

I was surprised at the numbness I felt and how few thoughts there were in my head. It was as if my brain just shut down, unable to process what I had witnessed. Looking back it was probably a blessing in disguise for my brain decided it had way too much emotion and closed the door on any more thoughts or emotions for the time being.

Dinner with his lawyer and prison minister was very relaxing and the conversation was about Mitch and the good times each of us had experienced. Sharing the experience and remembering the stories of better times reinforces the grief process.

Lunch the next day with the family was just as relaxing. Each family member took the time to thank me for all I had done for Mitch and how much it meant to them knowing someone was with him through the process. Each member asked for my contact information and I offered to speak with them anytime they had questions or concerns.

The biggest question on everybody's mind was did Mitch suffer? My explanation was simply I had not witnessed any discomfort on Mitch's face and believed he had passed peacefully. However the next day the media painted a completely different picture. A picture of suffocation, skin discoloration, muscle spasms, and chest heaving, all of these symptoms indicated a difficult suffocation.

I don't know what execution they witnessed but it was not the same execution I had witnessed by a long shot. I was furious they would print such a story just to sell papers; careless of the trauma it would cause the family.

My personal and professional opinion is any reporter sent to cover a story on death by lethal injection should be required to undergo at least forty hours of death and dying training. One young female witness for the prosecution never experienced the death of another human being and I thought she was either going to pass out, throw up, or both. How can a newspaper expect honest reporting from a reporter who had been so traumatized?

I know their version of the story sold a lot of newspapers and I guess that was their main goal. Again I question the lack of sensitivity for the family of the inmate.

Obviously the family called and questioned me intensely once the papers hit the streets. I calmly explained what had been reported was not what I had witnessed. I observed the area around his eyes, nose, mouth, his fingers and toes because pain inevitably causes involuntary twitching around the face, fingers, or feet and I saw nothing of the kind.

His jaw did quiver a little, and his stomach did spasm twice, but those were normal reactions to his body shutting down. I did not see any discoloration of the skin or signs of severe suffocation as stated in the paper, but then again I was being honest in my responses not trying to sell newspapers!

My mood driving home was amazingly calm and I didn't feel the least bit traumatized. This reaction, or lack of reaction, surprised me and I realized I was at peace with everything I had accomplished with Mitch. I hoped the family had the same calmness I was feeling and they would not only accept but also understand it was the feeling of closure on a long, painful, horrific story.

Yes Mitch was gone so now each member of the family could pick up the pieces and go on with their lives. Grief was surely going to surface again on holidays, anniversaries (especially the first anniversary of Mitch's execution), and family occasions. This was to be expected and I felt the family was well on their way to grieving in a very healthy way.

The family did hold a celebration of Mitch's life and it was a great way to share their grief and unintentionally take major strides in their own recovery.

I divided his ashes amongst the family members and disposed of some of his ashes in a manner he confided only to me. Fulfilling his request was the final step in my closure and gave me a feeling of pride and accomplishment. Would I ever do this again? If I were to be called, I knew I could do it again and do it successfully.

Chapter 32

Execution Summary

Now that I've taken you on my journey through death row and the execution let's review emotions and feelings of grief and bereavement.

1. Were you surprised at your own thoughts about executions?

2. Do you believe you could have taken this journey?

3. More importantly would you take such a journey if given the opportunity?

4. If you found yourself in my position would what you have read in this book that might be of any assistance?

5. What steps would you have shared with the family to assist them in preparing for the execution?

6. Do you feel you would be emotionally, personally, or professionally prepared for such a journey?

7. If the opportunity should arise, would you be able to put aside your personal feelings about the death penalty and work with an inmate and the family?

I want you not only to think about what you felt, but also I ask you to analyze your emotions as well. Not everyone could take such a journey and it would be OK to deny such a request.

Section Five

Another Murder Case

Chapter 33

A Father's Nightmare

I was having lunch with some friends when one of them asked if I had heard from an acquaintance of ours whom I hadn't seen for awhile. I confirmed I hadn't seen him lately but I didn't know if anything was wrong. The conversation at the table turned into a news room with all the reporters sharing their story and what they had been told, read, or seen on TV.

Apparently the son of the acquaintance was out bowling with his girlfriend and some friends when he got into a confrontation with a couple of men at a bowling alley. When push came to shove, they were all told to take it outside and as with any situation involving alcohol they did.

The son was challenged by a man much bigger than himself but was so afraid of losing face in front of his girl and buddies he didn't back down. According to all reports it was a one-sided fight that only took a couple of blows and was over.

The son was now humiliated in front of his girlfriend, buddies and anyone else watching the fight so he got in his pickup truck and called it a night or he should have.

According to the police report he dropped his girlfriend off at her house and instead of going home stopped at a drive thru and purchased a bottle of whiskey and a 12-pack of beer. He then drove back to the bowling alley and waited in the parking lot finishing off the alcohol.

As the place was closing he saw the man he thought he had the fight with earlier walking across the parking lot so he started his pickup truck and ran the man down. Once the man was down he backed over him killing him on the spot and just drove off.

Witnesses identified him and his truck to the police and the next morning he was arrested at home. His pickup truck was in the garage and still had the victims blood on the bumper and undercarriage of the truck.

The son admitted to being highly intoxicated and claimed he didn't remember a thing after dropping his girl off at her home. He verified he had been in a fight at the bowling alley the night before and the man he fought with was tall and had on a local team's sport jacket. After that he said he didn't remember much let alone running the man down in the parking lot.

To make matters worse the man he ran down and killed was not the man he had been in the fight with. The man he killed was an innocent victim who happened to be wearing the exact same team jacket. The man he fought with left the area minutes after the boy had left to take his girl home. The man he killed arrived an hour after the encounter and had no idea that anything had taken place let alone there was someone sitting in the parking lot getting smashed and waiting for revenge.

The son was charged with a long list of charges but the three main charges were premeditated murder, vehicular homicide, and assault with a deadly weapon with intent to kill. Any one of these three charges could bring life without parole but combined could bring the death penalty.

The tally of one night of drinking was as follows: One innocent victim dead, family and friends in total shock, a family's life in turmoil, and one life now destroyed.

The neighborhood and community were in denial and total disbelief since all involved were young hard-working well-respected and educated men. How could something like this happen in their neighborhood and the biggest question on everybody's minds was simply "How and why did this happen in the first place?"

142

Chapter 34

A Father's Guilt

There will be no closure to this story since the book will be finished before the son's story has an ending. I was hesitant to include it in this book but working with the father he felt if what he was experiencing could help another father or family I should include it in this book so here is what has happened to date.

I am not working with the son and don't know if I will since it is going to be several years before all the court proceedings are completed and he is sentenced. What I am including is the father's side of the story and what he and his family are going through as I write this section.

The rest of his comments will read more like an interview than a story line and that is exactly what it is. I will write about his experience with grief based on the notes he gave me permission to take and write into the book.

I will not mention names or places because you shall see society has already marked him and his family as failures and/or evil. You will witness how quickly society judges - - and without empathy.

At our first meeting I could tell he was extremely uncomfortable and nervous. When I asked him why he was so nervous he simply stated he wasn't used to talking to anyone other than his wife about his personal problems and she was just as traumatized as he was.

I asked if he was made more uncomfortable by talking to another man and if he would prefer to work with a woman. I know plenty of women who are professionals in the field and I could give him a recommendation if he felt it would be to his benefit.

He said working with me would be just fine, but he just didn't know where or how to start the conversation. I told him the best place to start was simply describing what he was feeling at that moment.

His uneasiness was based on the way he was raised. Like so many men in this country he was raised when trauma hit to just "man up" and get over it. This I believe is why so many men have such difficulty with grief and bereavement.

I started laughing (on purpose) and this angered him a little. When he ask what was so funny I simply stated that he was! It had been a long time since I had heard the term "man up" and told him I didn't think he was old enough to be so old school!

He grinned, relaxed a little more, and just shook his head. I told him I wouldn't be playing any games and there would be times he would want to punch me. But I knew him well enough to know how to approach certain emotions he would have to face and I was going to be blunt and not hold back on anything.

For example, I asked him about when he fell off his roof several years ago, was it an accident or just plain stupid? He said it was an accident and I said it was plain stupidity. When he asked me for an explanation I told him I knew he had enough training about roof repair to know when the slope of the roof was so steep you tied yourself off to something solid but he didn't.

He "manned up" and let his ego get in the way of common sense. When he hit the ground and broke his leg I questioned him if he "manned up" and set the broken bone himself, duck taped a 2x4 on his leg, and then got back on the roof? No, he called 911 and let medical professions set and repair his broken bone and took the amount of time required for it to heal properly.

With everything going on in his life he had to let go of the concept to "man up" and realize it was just like when he fell off the roof. Only this time I told him to think of it as if he landed on his head. He would need to call 911 and have medical professionals check him out.

The events which had taken place with his son were like falling off the roof. "You're broken up inside, you're heart is hurting, your

144

head is damaged, you can't focus, you can't think straight, your forgetting little things and driving yourself crazy." "You can't sleep because of the pain, your exhausted, not eating, losing weight, and cutting your wife and children out of you're life."

He wanted to be left alone but at the same time was afraid to be alone. He worried about the added bills, lawyers, court costs, and missing work at a time when he needed money the most.

"So damn it, quit trying to man up, find some professional help." I explained he couldn't do this alone and his wife and children needed him more than ever. He had to quit blaming himself for what his son had done and accept the fact there was nothing he could have done to prevent this tragedy.

If he insisted he had to "man up" then man up to the fact that burying his emotions was not the healthy way to go. Admitting his pain and being willing to show he was hurting to his wife and children meant being more of a man than trying to repress everything going on inside of him.

Men's emotions get hurt and the sooner they seek advice and get help the sooner they can get their life back. Don't think of this as a sign of weakness but more about a man who loved his wife and family so much and wanted to be there for them. Was he willing to take the amount of time, and do whatever it took, to heal properly?

This may not sound like a very professional approach but I knew him well enough that if I used all the politically correct and professional terminology there wouldn't be a second session. At the moment he needed a buddy more than a counselor.

I've discovered over the years when working with men the more you can describe things in terminology they understand and can relate to the more quickly they are going to respond to your help and advice.

Falling off the roof story was a perfect way to take a minor experience and turn it into a learning lesson he could understand and relate to. It was something which had already happened and he had recovered from it so now he could realize all the possibilities of recovering from this tragedy as well.

It may not seem like much but it took well over three hours to convey and what we did achieve was a trust and bond between us and he knew he could say anything to me and I would not pass judgment or ridicule him in any way. That was a lot to achieve in just three hours.

Chapter 35

A Father's Love for His Son

The next time we were together I could see the toll all of this was taking on his life and I insisted he tell me everything that was going on. This was the first of several meetings where I could see he was on the verge of breaking down and I gave him permission to do just that.

He wasn't a close friend but I knew him well enough that whenever he spoke about his son you could see the pride and love of a father in his eyes. They enjoyed sports together, hunted together, and during the summer months they often worked together. There was a tight bond between these two men and this bond was being tested to the extreme.

As we spoke, he told me how he tried everything he knew of to be a good father and I could read the doubts in his eyes. I took the opportunity to point out that he had done a terrific job of raising not only his son but his other children as well. He needed the reinforcement of knowing he was a good father and what had happened was his son's doing and not his. He wasn't there when it happened so there was no way he could have stopped it.

He was a hard working man and a good provider for his family. What else could a man expect of himself? They had a good life and a good home and he had done everything he could to raise his children to be responsible young adults.

He stated he felt if he had never let his son see him drink alcohol maybe this wouldn't have happened. Again I jumped in with it didn't matter if his son saw him drinking or not: his son would have learned to drink on his own. At least he never saw his father drunk or out of control so he did show his son there was responsibility when drinking.

He thought about his son's life growing up and how he never saw any warning signs of anger issues. How could his son have gotten so angry as to react in such a violent way? I explained he needed to accept the fact his son was way above the legal alcohol limit and under the cloud of alcohol people have done many insane things.

I asked him to make up a list of issues he was facing so we could go over them one by one and the following is what he came up with. I listed my responses after each question as I went through the list.

Q.   What more could he do for his son now his son was in jail and looking at life in prison or even the possibility of the death sentence.

A.   It was not the answer he wanted to hear but he needed to hear it. There was absolutely nothing he could do except continue to love his son and support him emotionally the best he could.

Q.   How much money would it take to get his son free?

A.   He could sell everything he owned and it still wouldn't be enough. There were eye witnesses and security videos so his son's guilt was beyond a shadow of a doubt. It was in the hands of the lawyers, jurors, and the court.

Q.   Did I think he should cash in all of his stocks and bonds, sell the house and whatever else he could to hire better attorneys?

A.   Having a more expensive lawyer was just wasting his money, future, and security for the rest of his family. It was an open and shut case and no lawyer in the world was going to be able to get his son set free no matter what he paid.

Q.   There had to be something he could do. The sitting around and waiting for the court hearings was driving him crazy.

A.   My advice was the best thing he could do was work with his wife and children in preparing them for what was to come. His children had been harassed at school for having a brother who was a killer. His wife was embarrassed to go to the store, church, or get her hair done. Even some of the men he worked with were not as supportive as he had anticipated.

Q.   Would his life ever return to normal?

A.   It depended on him and his wife and how they could make life better for his other children. His children were confused and scared because of the way society was reacting to them. They were afraid they could grow up to be killers. As parents their obligation was to their other children at home and helping them cope with everything that was going on.

Q.   He and his wife were having problems with intimacy, which had never been a problem before.

A.   Now was the time for him and his wife to seek professional counseling. They needed individual counseling, couple counseling, and family counseling. Everyone in the household was going to have unexpected issues and it was going to take a lot of time and patience to get everyone through this crisis.

Q.   He said it sounded as if I wanted him to forget his son whom he knew needed him now more than ever?

A.   No I was not suggesting for him to ignore his son and what was going on in his son's life. In order to help his son the most, he had to have a secure home base. He could not be of any assistance to his son if the rest of his life was in a shambles and running out of control.

Q. You've worked in prisons. What should I expect our lives to be like in the future?

A. Don't worry or concern yourself about the future. We will make those adjustments as they come along. His case would be tied up in court for several years so we had plenty of time to prepare and face those issues as they unfolded.

Q.   Would his life, their lives, ever be the same again?

A.   In all honesty, no way. Accept the fact the life he knew had been changed forever and would never be the same. Yes, he could, and would, with hard work be able to pull his life and family together again. It would be a different life and there would be unexpected changes in his life's routine but he could experience a happy family life again if they all work together to achieve this one goal.

Q.   When people ask me about what happened the night my son took another mans life what do I tell them.

A.   The answer was all up to him. Was it someone asking so they may offer help or was it someone just trying to stir up issues? How he would respond should be determined by who was asking. There was nothing wrong with simply stating he was not comfortable discussing it at the time and change the subject. If the person persisted simply smile and walk off or leave if necessary. He was not under any obligation to repeat the story to every Tom, Dick, or Harry trying to pry into his family's personal life.

Q.   How do I handle the media when they call or confront me outside my place of business or home?

A.   Tell them if they had any questions to speak with your son's lawyer and that you have nothing to say. Obtain legal restrictions on how close they can get to your home, his children's schools, and place of employment. Realize in time the story will cool off and they won't be there anymore unless something they deem newsworthy happens in court. Then you can expect to find them out front again but you still are not required to give anyone a statement. If you discover they are harassing your children file a complaint with your district attorney and ask the school to restrict any media contact with your children.

Q.   What do I tell my youngest when she asks where her brother is?

A.   Again, this would be his call. As her father, how much information did he think she needed at the time? Did he feel he could comfort her without giving her too many details until she was older? Sitting down and speaking with his other children was imperative so he could explain how they had to be careful about conversations with their friends and not to email, blog, text, face book or tweet any of their personal or family information especially during the trial. It is too easy for the media and anyone else out there to track such conversations. I couldn't stress this enough for the protection of all involved.

* * *

All of this took place over several meetings and I'm happy to report the family is receiving professional help and doing as well as can be expected. I hope to continue working with the father in preparing him and his family for the upcoming prison visitations and what to expect once we have the final verdict and sentencing.

Chapter 36

Analysis & Conclusion

I want to review this case by breaking it down into the stages we discussed in the beginning of the book.

SHOCK – Can you imagine the shock you would experience by having the police show up at your house with warrants for the arrest of your son? One warrant for his vehicle, one for the clothes he was wearing the night before, and the most devastating of all, a murder warrant for his arrest. This is something none of us would ever expect in our lifetime but here is an all-American hard-working family having to face such an issue.

PREOCCUPATION – He mentioned in our first meeting he could not concentrate on work, was forgetting simple things, finding himself standing in a room and not remembering why he was there. Mentally reviewing his son's childhood and analyzing everything he could to see what he as a father could have done differently to prevent this. These are the classic signs of preoccupational grief such as wanting to stop the events before they took place or changing one small detail in his son's history with hopes of once again changing what had happened.

SYMPTOMS – He and his wife displayed all of the following symptoms: sleeplessness, a choking feeling, shortness of breath, an empty hollow feeling, digestive symptoms, poor appetite, unexplained simple aches and pains, and as I mentioned before trouble concentrating. Here were the classic symptoms of a couple in the throws of grief.

His children had classic grieving symptoms such as: withdrawing from their friends, declining school performance, reports of aggressive and unrestrained play, and the eldest refused to go to school and wanted to change schools, and all of them started engaging in games based on death or dying.

HOSTILE REACTIONS – With the lack of intimacy between him and his wife they were starting to experience more and more hostility with each other. They were less tolerant of their children's behavior and became easily angered by their friends, co-workers, and neighbors. The biggest surprise of all was when they both realized just how much anger they held for their son whose actions had put the entire family in the middle of the nightmare.

WITHDRAWAL – As I mentioned above his wife stopped going to church, hated shopping, and canceled her hair appointments because of fear of what conversations would arise at the salon.

He discovered he was spending more and more time in the garage and not with his wife and children. His behavior became what I call self incarceration. He had developed the inability to interact with anyone, was denying the reality of the situation, and avoided major issues by trying to hide in his own little world.

His children would come home from school and go directly to their rooms avoiding contact with other family members, neighbors, and friends.

Withdrawal and isolation are very dangerous for young adults and children since this isolation could lead to suicidal thoughts or actions.

LIVING WITHOUT – Everyone in the family including the extended family would have to learn to live without the son being a major part of their social lives and family functions. As I have mentioned throughout this book, living without due to incarceration can be devastating because of the loss of the individual's participation in the family's daily activities.

* * *

I know from experience what the future holds for this family. They will need to stay with their counseling sessions, as all of them are walking a very thin line at the time of writing this book. I hope they survive the challenges which lie ahead of them and their son, and I pray they find peace and happiness in their future.

Additional Grief Resources

The following resources were adapted from the GriefWork Network Resource Manual, and used here by permission.

Audio CDs

Relaxation Visualization by Dan Newman (ceucert.com)

Grief Bereavement Visualization by Dan Newman (ceucert.com)

We Live on Borrowed Time by Paul Alexander (paulalexander.-com)

Before Their Time: Memorial Songs and Music (beforetheirtime.-com)

In Memory Of by Marcie O'Neil

Books of General Interest

Tuesdays with Morrie: An old man, a young man & life's greatest lesson, Mitch Albom, 1997. Highlights the relationship that a dying professor has with one of his former students. They met on Tuesday's and discussed the importance of life. The professor dies from ALS (Lou Gerhig's disease) Based on a true story.

Don't Ask for the Dead Man's Golf Clubs: What to do and say (and what not to say) when a friend loses a loved one. Lynn Kelly, 2000 This book takes a humorous approach to help others know what to say and do when a loved one or friend's life is touched by death.

The Jewish Way in Death & Mourning, Maurice Lamm, 1969. Explains Jewish tradition related to death and the grieving process. Easy to follow for those who want to understand more fully the Jewish tradition.

Letting Go-Reflections on Dying, Morrie Schwartz, 1996. Reflections by Morrie Schwartz who was a college professor. He was diagnosed with ALS-Lou Gerhig's disease and he faced his death with courage, wit and wisdom. Very inspirational.

The Art of Condolence: What to write, What to say, What to do at a time of loss, Leonard & Hilary Zunin, 1991. Provides insightful ways to express feelings and thoughts when someone experiences a death. A nice reference book for those who work in the field of bereavement.

Planning Memorial Celebrations, Rob Baker, 1999. Provides helpful suggestions for services immediately following a death as well as services that occur at a later time.

Six Simple Weeks: A Caring Manual for Support Group Leaders, Eloise Cole and Joy Johnson, 2001. This book is based on a six week bereavement support group model. Provides helpful hints on how to begin a group and how to structure each week.

Holiday Hope: Remembering Loved Ones During Special Times of the Year, Fairway Press, 1998. This book provides helpful hints on how to deal with all the special holidays that occur during the year after the death of a loved one, including anniversaries, birthdays, etc.

Effective Support Groups: How to plan, design, facilitate and enjoy them, James Miller, 1998. Provides many help suggestions on how to start and facilitate a bereavement support group.

Death & Grief: Healing Through Group Support, Harold Ivan Smith, 1995. This book walks leaders and participants through a healing group experience. This book provides religious references for those interested in providing a church group.

Holiday Help: A Guide for Hope & Healing, Darcie Sims and Sherry Williams, 1996. Simple activities to help families cope with the holidays.

How To Start and Lead a Bereavement Support Group, Alan Wolfert; 1997. Provides a "step-by-step" approach to starting and facilitating a bereavement support group.

Books for Adults

How to Survive the Loss of a Parent: A Guide for Adults, Lois F. Akner, 1993. This book is based on a bereavement support group. Each participant lost a parent in his/her adult years. Helps adults deal with the death of a parent.

Nobody's Child Anymore: Grieving, Caring & Comforting when Parents Die, Barbara Bartocci, 2000. This book talks about the issues adults face when the last parent dies. Provides helpful insight to unexpected feelings that arise within adults as they mourn their loss.

Last Touch: Preparing for a Parent's Death, Marilyn R. Becker, 1992. Addresses the issues related to an adult who lost a parent. It includes several stories from adult children who have experienced the death of a parent.

Early Winter, Howard Bronson, 1995. Beautifully written by a man whose father died unexpectedly. He discusses the feelings that are brought out during the grieving process. A good book especially from a male perspective.

Midlife Orphan: Facing Changes Now That Your Parents Are Gone, Jane Brooks, 1999. No matter how old we are, losing a parent hurts. This book addresses the feelings many adults face when they experience the death of their parents, especially when both parents are deceased.

Dying Well: Peace & Possibilities at the End-Of-Life, Ira Byock, MD 1997. This book helps patients and their families deal with end-of-life issues with dignity and hope.

Grief's Courageous Journey: A Workbook, Sandi Caplan & Gordon Lang, 1995. Excellent book to use with an adult client as they work through the grieving process. Helps them identify feelings, emotions, etc. through writing, drawing and discussion.

Final Gifts: Understanding the special awareness, needs & communications of the dying, Maggie Callahan & Patricia Kelley, 1992. This book provides understanding of the special needs and concerns of those who are dying and ways to be supportive.

Father Loss: How sons of all ages come to terms with the death of their dads, Neil Chethik, 2001. Discusses the issues that men deal with when their fathers die and how others can support them.

At Home With Dying: A Zen Hospice Approach, Merrill Collett, 1997. Provides guidance for the caregiver to help a loved one die at home.

In Lieu of Flowers: A conversation with the living, Nancy Cobb, 2000. This book addresses ways the grieving can deal with their grief by finding support from family and friends. Insightful and encouraging.

Chicken Soup for the Surviving Soul: 101 stories of Courage & Inspiration Cranfield, Hansen, Aubery & Mitchell, 1996. Short, easy to read, inspirational stories written by individuals who have survived tragedy or death.

Chicken Soup for the Grieving Soul: Stories about Life, Death & Overcoming the Loss of a Loved One, Cranfield, Hansen, 2003. Short, easy to read, inspirational stories written by individuals who have survived death of a loved one.

Give Sorrow Words-A Father's Passage through Grief, Tom Crider, 1996. Provides insight on how one father dealt with the grief of losing his only daughter who was an adult when she died. He talks about the importance of "owning the grief" and talking about it.

Recovering from the Loss of a Loved One to AIDS - Help for surviving family, friends, and lovers who grieve, Katherine Fair Donnelly, 1994. Written for those who know the pain and isolation of losing a loved one to AIDS. Sensitively written and addresses the special grief related to death by this disease.

Motherless Daughters , Hope Edelman, 1994. Written by a woman whose mother died of breast cancer, she addresses issues that women may face as they deal with being motherless. Good book for adult women who have lost a mother, at any age, to death.

Letters From Motherless Daughters , Hope Edelman, 1995. As a follow-up to her first book, Hope captures letters that she has received from women who discuss being motherless. Very moving and may be helpful to clients by encouraging them to write about their mothers.

Companion Through the Darkness: Inner Dialogues on Grief, Stephanie Ericsson; 1993. The book is written by a young widow and provides short inspirational reflections on the issues one faces while grieving. A good book for young widows.

Living With A Man Who Is Dying, Jocelyn Evans, 1971. This is a personal memoir in tribute to her husband and the journey they traveled in his illness and death.

Later Courtney , Susan Evans, 1997. Written by a mother who lost her 22-year old daughter in an auto accident. Entries from a journal over a year's time.

I'm Grieving As Fast As I Can: How Young Widows & Widowers Can Cope and Heal, Linda Feinberg, 1994. Written for young widows/widowers, addresses many of the issues that they face. Looks at the ways their lives have been altered by the death, from raising young children to meeting new people. Good book for someone who is young and widowed.

When Winter Follows Spring: Surviving the death of an adult child, Dorothy Ferguson . This book addresses the unique pain that parents endure when an adult child dies. Provides helpful hints on how to cope with this type of loss.

Death & Dying or Can You Love Me Enough to Let Me Go, Bruce A. Foster, 1997. This easy to read storybook is for adults who struggle with letting go of their loved one. The book is written by a son who experienced the struggle with his father's death.

Storytelling in Bereavement, Alida Gersie, 1991. This book utilizes storytelling to help understand and deal with grief.

Widow To Widow, Genevieve Ginsburg, 1995. Written for widows, this book addresses many practical issues they face in adjusting to their new life. Practical and easy to read.

Swallowed by a Snake, Thomas R. Golden, 2000. This book addresses the masculine side of grief and healing. This book includes storytelling and cross-cultural aspects related to male grief.

A Time to Say Good-Bye: Moving Beyond Loss , Mary McClure Goulding, 1996. Written by a social worker who is also a widow. She addresses issues related to the dying process, the funeral and adjusting to life without your loved one.

Living When A Loved One Has Died, Earl A. Grollman, 1977. This book is written in poetry form and addresses feelings related to death.

Companion to Grief, Patricia Kelley, 1997. Addresses issues related to grief, including workplace grief, helping someone who is grieving and starting new relationships.

The Courage to Laugh: Humor, Hope and Healing in the Face of Death and Dying, Allen Klein, 1998. Written for those who are or have faced the reality of death in their lives. Provides hope and ways to find humor in the face of sadness. Inspirational.

Grandma's Tears-Comfort for Grieving Grandparents, June Cerza Kolf, 1995. Written for any grandparent who has lost a grandchild. Deals with issues and feelings experienced by the grieving grandparent and helps to explain what their adult child must be experiencing.

166

To Live Until We Say Good-bye, Elisabeth Kubler-Ross, 1978. Moving story about the lives of several dying individuals and how they lived their lives through the dying process. Captured in word and with pictures, this book is an inspiration to those who are dying as well as living.

On Death & Dying , Elisabeth Kubler-Ross, 1968 The original book about death and dying..

The Wheel of Life, Elisabeth Kubler-Ross, 1997. Ross's memoirs on living and dying. Traces her life, including the years she has struggled with her own illnesses and her reactions to "dying."

When Bad Things Happen to Good People, Harold S. Kushner, 1989. Written for all those good people who have experienced bad things in their lives. May be helpful for those who don't understand why "this happened to me."

Acknowledgment: Opening to the grief of unacceptable loss, Peter Leech & Zeva Singer, 1988. Acknowledges the feelings and loss associated with a death and provides different ways to work through the grief.

Grandfather Remembers - Memories for my Grandchildren, Judith Levy, 1987. This book provides the guidelines for grandfathers to provide information that they would like to leave their grandchild. A wonderful way for grandparents to leave a sense of family history, relevant facts and fun information for future generations.

Grandmother Remembers - A Written Heirloom for my Grandchildren, Judith Levy, 1986, *See Grandfather Remembers*.

Doors Close, Doors Open: Widows, Grieving & Growing, Morton Lieberman, 1996. Written for women who have lost their spouse, this book presents common experiences, feelings, etc. that women experience when they become "widowed."

Gathering a Life: A journey of recovery, Jeanne Lohmann, 1989. This book was written by the wife of a cancer patient. She uses

167

short stories to address their struggles to survive his illness and his death. The book helps families identify with the struggles and the grief.

Don't Take My Grief Away from Me, Doug Manning . Addresses the issues of grief and the importance of allowing others to grieve the death of their loved one instead of "minimizing" the loss.'

Losing A Parent - A personal guide to coping with that special grief that comes with losing a parent, Fiona Marshall, 1993. This book is written for adult children who have lost a parent. It covers all types of death from illness to sudden death. Presents real life situations and discusses reactions, feelings, etc.

I Can't Stop Crying, John D. Martin & Frank D. Ferris, 1992. Written for those who have lost a spouse or partner. Captures many of the feelings and emotions that a widow/widower or surviving partner may experience.

I Don't Know HOW to Help Them, Linda Maurer, 1996. Written by a woman who lost her only child, she provides helpful hints for family members and friends to help bereaved parents.

A Broken Heart Still Beats, Anne McCracken & Mary Semel, 1998. A book for parents who have lost a child. Written by two wo-men who have lost children.

Gentle Closings Companion: Questions & Answers for Coping With The Death of Someone You Love, Ted Menten, 2002. This book helps you find the way to say "good-bye" to someone you love that is dying.

After Goodbye, Ted Menten, 1994. This book helps adults continue on with their life after the death of a loved one. Good for anyone who has lost a loved one.

The Caregiver's Companion: Words to Comfort & Inspire, Betty Clare Moffatt, 2000. An uplifting collection of inspirational essays interviews and advise for those who provide care for others.

168

When Parents Die, Edward Myers, 1997. Addresses many different aspects of a death of a parent, from funeral arrangements and estate settlements to coping with life without a parent. Includes issues related to sudden death and suicide as well as illness.

How We Die: Reflections on Life's Final Chapter, Sherwin B. Nuland, 2003. Discusses ways that people die and provides insight on who to live life more fully and meaningfully.

More Than Surviving - Caring for yourself while you grieve, Kelly Osmont, 1990. This is a short booklet that discusses the need to move beyond one's grief. It is feminist in its approach and much directed. (Review prior to use with a client)

Dying At Home: A family guide for caregiving, Andrea Sankar, 1999. Based on the experience of those who have cared for a loved one at home who was dying. Helpful and supportive information.

The TAO of Dying: A Guide to Caring, Doug Smith, 1997. Provides inspiration to those who are dying as well as those who care for them.

Grieving The Death of a Friend, Herald Ivan Smith, 1996. Losing a friend is one of the most significant but unrecognized experiences of grief. This book addresses the special grief that grieving friend's experience.

On Grieving the Death of a Father, Herald Ivan Smith, 1994. This book addresses the issues that adult children face when their father dies. Includes adults who lost their fathers as teenagers.

How to say Goodbye: Working through personal grief, Joanne Smith & Judy Biggs, 1990. Provides helpful information about dealing with the death of a loved one.

Beyond Grief, Carol Staudacher, 1987. Discusses issues related to grief and coping mechanisms. This book addresses many types of loss including spouse, parent, child, accidental death and suicide. Affirms feelings related to loss.

Men and Grief, A guide for men surviving the death of a loved one, Carol Staudacher, 1991.This book explores grief from the male perspective. The book discusses reaction to death, how they are "supposed" to react and how they react internally. Provides valuable insight on male grief.

A Time to Grieve: Meditations for healing after the death of a loved one , Carol Staudacher, 1994. This book has beautiful meditations related to loss and feelings.

The Courage to Grieve, Judy Tatelbaum, 1984. Generic to any type of grieving. Excellent book for clients.

You Don't Have to Suffer, Judy Tatelbaum, 1990. A handbook for moving beyond life's crisis. The book provides insight on how previous losses in one's life may cause a barrier to dealing with a current crisis. A good book for those who are about a year removed from the death and appear to be stuck in their grief process.

I Remember...I Remember, Enid Samuel Traisman, 1992. A keepsake journal for adults. A simple, beautiful way for memories, feelings, and other thoughts to be recorded.

The Death of a Wife: Reflections for a grieving husband, Robert Vogt, 1996. Written for men who have lost a spouse. Written by a man who struggled with the pain of emptiness and loss after his wife died.

When There Are No Words - Finding your way to cope with loss & grief, Charlie Walton, 1996. Written by a parent who lost two young adult children two weeks before Christmas. Their deaths were accidental but drugs played a role. Male grief and the impact on the family are discussed.

Good Grief, Granger E. Westberg, 1971. This concise book discusses the loss of a loved one and may help people deal with everyday losses.

Anticipatory Grief: Living With Grief When Illness is Prolonged, Kenneth J. Doka, Ph.D., 1997. Presents several brief articles on different types of illness that might prolong the grieving process such as Alzheimer's, ALS, Cancer, Etc. Good reference book if preparing a presentation for caregivers.

Books about Cancer and Grief

Healing Essence ,Mitchell Gaynor, 1995. A cancer doctor's practical program for hope and recovery.

Living Beyond Breast Cancer, Marisa & Ellen Weiss, 1997. Written as a survivor's guide for when treatment ends and the rest of your life begins. Addresses issues many breast cancer patients and their families face.

Coping With Cancer, John Packo, 1991. Twelve creative choices for those dealing with cancer. This is a scripture based approach to healing.

Gilda's Disease, Steven Piver, 1996. Written by a doctor who provides a medical perspective on ovarian cancer. Includes the personal experience of Gene Wilder based and his wife, Gilda Radner.

Diagnosis Cancer: Your Guide to the First Few Months, Wendy Schessel Harpham, MD, 1998. Written by a physician and cancer survivor, provides helpful hints in a question and answer format.

After Cancer: A Guide to Your New Life, Wendy Schlessel Harpham, MD, 1994. Provides practical advise and helpful hints for cancer patients and/or their loved ones related to life after a cancer diagnosis.

When A Parent Has Cancer, Wendy Schessel Harpham, MD, 1997. This book is a guide for parents who also have cancer. This book would be valuable for anyone working with children who are dealing with cancer in their family.

Books for Children & Adolescents

When I'm Afraid , Jane Aaron, 1998. Short, easy to read book that helps children understand the fear of being afraid & what they can do when they are afraid. Good for use by professionals working with young children. Pre-school-elementary.

When I'm Angry, Jane Aaron & Barbara Gardiner, 1998. Short, easy to read book that helps children understand what they can do when they are angry. Good for use by parents or professionals working with young children. Helps them identify and discuss feelings. Pre-school-elementary.

Someone Special is Very Sick, Jim & Joan Boulden, 1995. Workbook written for younger children to help them deal with the serious illness of someone special.

When I Die, Will I Get Better?, Joeri & Piet Breebaart, 1993.Beautifully written story about illness & death in terms young children can understand. Instead of children, the Rabbit family is featured. Preschool-elementary age children.

Bye, Mis' Lela , Dorothy Carter, 1998. Story about a caregiver who dies. Helps children understand death. Features African-American children & adults. Elementary age group.

Everett Anderson's Goodbye , Lucille Cliford, 1983. Describes how a little boy feels after his father dies. Good book for elementary students to read or to be read to pre-school children. The family is African-American and appropriate for a culturally diverse group.

I Had A Friend Named Peter , Janice Cohn; 1987. This book helps children understand the death of a friend their age. Age appropriate for pre-school-elementary school. There is a summary of information for parents and educators.

I'm Mad , Elizabeth Crary, 1992. Written for primary grades to help children deal with their anger.

Just A Heartbeat Away,When A Mother Dies of AIDS , Gabriel Constans, 1996. A story book to use with children who are dealing with a death of a loved one related to AIDS. In the book, it seems that the mother dies rather quickly after her diagnosis. This might be difficult for children who watched their loved one die a slow death. Ages middle to junior high.

I'm Scared , Elizabeth Crary, 1994. Written for primary grades to help children deal with their feelings of being afraid. Elementary school age.

Boogeyman in the Basement , Kathleen Duey & Ron Berry. Helps children confront their fears in a safe way. Elementary school age.

Nana Upstairs & Nana Downstairs , Tomie dePaola, 1973. Multi-generation family deals with the death of a great-grandma. Elementary school age.

Glad Monster, Sad Monster , Ed Emberley & Anne Miranda, 1997. Book helps children talk about feelings. The book has fold-out masks for use by children to help them talk about their feelings.

Holidays & Special Days , Jessie Flynn, 1994. Storybook with suggestions to help young children celebrate special occasions after the death of a loved one. Preschool to elementary age.

Sophie , Mem Fox, 1994. A story about life & death. A little African-American girl comes to understand life & death when her grandfather dies. Preschool-elementary age children.

Good Grief: Helping Groups of Children When A Friend Dies , Sandra S. Fox. Written for those who work with children. The book provides activities to facilitate group discussion and things to look for that might indicate a need to refer the child or children for additional counseling.

Part of Me Died, Too: Stories of Creative Survival Among Bereaved Children & Teens, Virginia Lynn Fry, 1995. Discusses ways children and teens survived the death of a loved one. Includes death of father, mother, grandparent, pet, and friend and includes deaths from AIDS, murder, suicide and illness.

Beyond the Ridge , Paul Goble; 1993. A short story about death based on Indian legacy. Comforting story that could be read to pre-school to elementary age children.

When A Friend Dies: A book for teens about grieving & healing , Marilyn Gootman, 1994. Simply & concisely discusses teen grief and ways for them to heal. Answers common questions & addresses fears and feelings. Appropriate for Jr. /Sr. High.

Talking About Death , Earl & Sharon Grollman. Workbook to help children deal with a death. An aid for parents or professionals who are working with a grieving child. Elementary school age.

The Next Place , Warren Hanson, 1997. Easy to read book that shares what "the next life" will be like, an imaginary journey. Good for use of primary-middle school age children as well as adults.

When Something Terrible Happens - Children can learn to cope with grief , Marge Heegaard; 1991. This journal for children helps them identify and discuss their feelings. It allows them to draw and write about their feelings. For young children.

When Someone Very Special Dies , Marge Heegaard; 1988. This journal assists young children in identifying and talking about their grief. It allows them to draw and write about their feelings.

When Someone Has a Very Serious Illness.Marge Heegaard, 1991. This journal assists young children in identifying and talking about their fears when someone they love is very ill.

The Brightest Star , Kathleen Maresh Hemery, 1998. Story about a young girl whose mother died. She struggles with defining her family without her mother when she has a school project to complete. Appropriate for elementary-middle school.

Losing Uncle Tim , Mary Kate Jordan, 1989. This book addresses a death related to AIDS and is geared towards elementary to middle school age children. Deals with the feelings a child has when they lose a family member to AIDS.

Kathy's Hats , Trudy Krisher, 1992. Story of a young girl who gets sick and needs chemotherapy. She losses her hair and finds comfort in the variety of hats that she can wear. Elementary-middle school age children.

How It Feels When A Parent Dies , Jill Krementz 1981. This book is written with stories from children who explain how they felt when they lost a parent. A very inspirational book for use with middle-high school age children/teens.

What is a feeling? , David W. Krueger, MD, 1993. Multicultural book that helps children identify feelings and talk about them. Elementary-middle school age.

Daddy's Chair , Sandy Lanton, 1991. Written for young children who have lost a parent, especially a father. Explains Jewish tradition related to death and helps a young boy deal with his father's death from cancer.

For Those Who Live -Helping children cope with the death of a brother or sister, Kathy LaTour; 1983/1991. This book talks about the grieving that occurs when a child or young adult dies in a family. It deals with the different feelings that might be experienced and how family dynamics might change. Middle to Junior High school level.

Learning to Say Good-Bye When a Parent Dies. Eda LeShan; 1976. This book seems appropriate for middle-junior high children. Addresses issues such as "what about me?"; "the fear of being left alone" and many other thoughts.

Forever In My Heart , Jennifer LeVine, 1992. A story that helps children participate in life as a parent dies. Integrates story- telling and art to help the child deal with his loss. Elementary school age.

Liplap's Wish , Jonathan London; 1994. A storybook about death for children. Age appropriate for pre-school to elementary.

Why Did Grandma Die? , Trudy Madler; 1980. This is a story about the death of a grandmother and the effect it had on her school age granddaughter. Elementary to middle school age children.

On the Wings of a Butterfly , Marilyn Maple, 1992. A story about life & death. Young girl has cancer & dies but she comes to understand her life & death by the meaning of butterflies. Middle school age children.

Listen for the Fig Tree , Sharon Bell Mathis, 1974. Story about an African-American teenager who must deal with the death of her father & her mother's grief. Written as a novel, deals with poverty, blindness and aspects of grief. Appropriate for Jr/Sr high.

Lifetimes: The Beautiful Way to Explain Death to Children , Byron Mellonie & Robert Ingpen; 1983. This story book tells of the life and death cycle through the use of story and pictures. Appropriate for pre-school-elementary age children.

Aarvy Aarvark Finds Hope , Donna O'Toole; 1988. The book addresses life, friendship and death. Elementary to middle school age children will enjoy this book.

Mommy's in the Hospital Again , Carolyn Stearns Parkinson, 1996. Discusses the feelings a young boy experiences as his mother deals with a chronic illness. The family helps him deal with his feelings about "Mom being sick." K-5th grade.

When A Pet Dies , Fred Rogers, 1988. Help children understand the death of pet by a story. Preschool-elementary age children.

A Birthday Present for Daniel , Juliet Rothman, 1996. Beautiful story about a young child whose brother died. Captures changes that occur in a family when a child dies. Elementary-middle school age children.

Love, Mark , Mark Scrivani; 1988. This book is written for children in letter form, answers questions related to grief. Elementary to junior high age.

Love, Mark II , Mark Scrivani; 1990. Builds on Love, Mark. See above .

What's Wrong with Grandma? , Margaret Shawver, 1996. A story about a family who learns to deal with Grandma's Alzheimer's disease. Helps children understand about memory loss and the disease. Middle-junior high school.

What's Heaven? - Written for the child who has lots of questions about "life after death" and where people & animals go when they die. Written for pre-school-elementary children.

The Saddest Time , Norma Simon, 1986. Summarizes several types of death, how children were told and how they handled the death. A story book for elementary children.

After Charlotte's Mom Died , Cornelia Spelman, 1996. Addresses the pain and loneliness that a young girl feels after her Mom died. Her Dad is grieving and she doesn't know how to help or where to turn. After a fight at school, the girl & her father seek guidance from a therapist to help them deal with their grief. Elementary to middle school age.

See you in Heaven , Rev. Joe Stripling, 1998. When a little boy is diagnosed with cancer, he searches for the meaning of God. Written from a faith perspective. Appropriate for pre-school-elementary.

Fire in My Heart, Ice in My Veins: A journal for teenagers experiencing a loss , Enid Samuel Traisman; 1992. This is a journal that

180

will assist teenagers in recognizing and owning their feelings related to loss. Early to mid teens would benefit from this journal.

Dear Bruno , Alice Trillin, 1996. A sick dinosaur tries to cheer up a fellow dinosaur that has cancer. A book of hope and helpful hints for the young who are dealing with cancer. Elementary-middle school age.

Saying Goodbye to Daddy , Judith Vigna, 1991. A story book for pre-school to elementary age children. A little girl mourns the death of her father.

To Hell With Dying , Alice Walker; 1988. This book features African-American children and their family members. The book is written from the perspective of a young woman who was deeply touched by a neighbor and his love for children in the neighborhood. It is a book of hope. Middle to junior high school age children.

Cool Cats, Calm Kids , Mary Williams, 1996. Relaxation & stress management for young children. Helpful hints for to help teach children about relaxation. Elementary-middle school age.

Red Ribbon , Sarah Weeks, 1995. Book & audio tape about a young girl who learns about the meaning of a red ribbon when a neighbor becomes ill. This book could be helpful for adults to discuss AIDS with children. Elementary-middle school age.

After the Funeral , Jane Loretta Winsch, 1995. Multicultural book to help children understand their feelings after the loss of someone significant in their live. Encourages children to share their thoughts, feelings & fears. Preschool-elementary school age children.

We Don't Like to Remember Them as a Field of Grass: A book by children who have had a loved one murdered - From the Dougy Center, 1991. A simple workbook to help children deal with a death when a loved one was murdered. Workbook style integrates storytelling & pictures to share their loss.

Books for Parents

Explaining Death to Children , Earl Grollman; 1967. This book is written for parents and professionals who work with children. Provides information on the stages of understanding by children based on their age.

Talking About Death , Earl Grollman, 1990. Written for parents or those who work with children. Addresses ways that death can be discussed with children.

How Do We Tell The Children? A Parents Guide to Helping Children Understand and Cope When Someone Dies , Dan Schaefer & Christine Lyons 1987. This book assists parents in discussing death with their children.

The Bereaved Parent , Harriet Sarnoff Schiff; 1977. This book is written for parents who have lost a child. It addresses many of the problems and challenges they will face as they deal with the death of their child.

Books for Professionals

Author's Note: These professional reference books are particularly well-suited for use by professionals when approaching grief. Several contain excellent structured plans for conducting groups and workshops. Please note, however, that some may have sensitive content requiring professional context and guidance. As such, please review any of these books carefully before recommending.

Disenfranchised Grief: Recognizing Hidden Grief , Ken Doka, 1989. Discusses the various types of losses that may not be recognized due to relationships shared by the person who died and the griever. Helpful for professionals.

Windows: Healing & Helping Through Loss, Mary Jo Hannaford & Michael Popkin, 1992. A program with client handbooks, leader guide, other media.

Beyond the Innocence of Childhood: Helping Children & Adolescents Cope with Life-Threatening Illness and Dying, David Adams & Eleanor Deveau 1995. Three-book series that addresses many issues children and teenagers face as they deal with illness and death. Insightful and useful information related to development and age-appropriate discussions.

The Art of Healing - Childhood Grief: School based expressive arts program, Anne Black & Penelope Simpson Adams; 1993. Usable ideas for helping children express their feelings through art. Includes a facilitator's guide and offers 4 different sections related to specific issues. Offers a step-by-step process to facilitate grief counseling within a school setting.

The Last Dance: Encountering Death & Dying, Lynne Despelda & Albert Strickland, 1999. Provides valuable information on various cultures and how they view death. Good resource book.

The Path Ahead: Reading in Death & Dying, Lynne Despelda & Albert Strickland, 2003. A collection of short articles related to death & dying. Articles include multicultural, social issues, medical ethics & decision making, violence, suicide, & personal dimensions of loss. Good reference book.

Children Mourning, Mourning Children, Kenneth Doka; 1995. Excellent book for professionals to use in dealing with the many aspects and ways children mourn. Good for school counselors. Includes a helpful bibliography.

Living With Grief: At Work, At School, At Worship, Kenneth Doka, 1999. Addresses the issues of loss in various settings and the impact grief has in all aspects of our lives.

Living With Grief: Who We Are; How We Grieve, Kenneth Doka & Joyce Davidson; 1998. Provided by the Hospice Foundation of America, this book explores grief from various perspectives including religious believes, ethnic backgrounds, socio-economic situations as well as helping those with developmental disabilities. A good reference book for understanding various & diverse groups.

Fernside Idea Book: A Guidebook for Group Facilitators, Fernside, a Center for Grieving Children. This practical guidebook provides ideas for groups, activities, etc.

Afraid to Ask: A book for families to share about Cancer, Judylaine Fine, 1986. Provides easy to understand information about cancer & treatments. Also provides easy to understand explanations of several types of cancer. Good for use with families & children in a family session or with adults to share with their children. Information about the various types of cancer may be valuable to share with clients & their families.

Coping When a Parent Has AIDS, Barbara Draimin; 1993. Provides helpful information to assist children & teenagers deal with AIDS in their family.

The Grieving Child , Helen Fitzgerald; 1992. This book is a guide for educators and parents. It addresses anticipatory grief as well as life after a death has occurred in a family.

Bereaved Children & Teens , Earl Grollman; 1995. This book is an excellent support guide for professionals and parents. The book is divided into 3 major sections, each dealing with age-appropriate issues, including religious traditions.

Straight Talk about Death for Teenagers, Earl Grollman; 1993. This book is for teenagers but would compliment group or individual counseling. It may help the teen identify some areas of concern and generate questions.

Bereavement Support Group Program for Children, Beth Haasl & Jean Marnocha; 1990. This is a leader's guide for facilitating a support group for children who are mourning. Provides ideas for topics and projects to assist with group discussion.

A Child Shall Lead Them-Lessons in Hope From Children With Cancer , Diane Komp, MD, 1993. Integrates stories of children with cancer with biblical hope and modern medicine. Inspirational stories for those who work with children with chronic or terminal illnesses.

Lucy Lettuce, Patrick Loring & Joy Johnson, 1994. This book uses "puns" to tell a story of grief and recovery. Great to use with children as well as adults. Therapeutic use of storytelling.

How to Help Children Through a Parent's Serious Illness , Kathleen McCue, 1994. A valuable resource for professionals to share with families who have children and want to help them deal with a serious illness in their family. Provides ways to share information, integrate children into the process, etc.

Facing Changes: Falling apart & coming together again in the teen years , Donna O'Toole, 1995. Addresses issues of grief & loss by providing information and questions for the teen to answer related to their loss. Practical guide for use in a classroom or support group setting. Professionals working with teens.

Tear Soup: A recipe for healing after loss, Pat Schweibert & Chuck DeKlyen, 1999. This is a story book that can be used with adults as well as children. Provides great insight on the emotions experienced by the bereaved. A great teaching tool to use with professionals or in groups.

Interventions with Bereaved Children, Susan C. Smith & Sr. Margaret Pennells, 1995. Guide for parents & professionals working with children who are grieving. Assists with chronic or terminal illness and death.

Bereavement: It's Pyschosocial Aspects, Schoenberg, Gerber, Wiener, Kutscher, Peretz & Carr; 1977. This book provides a clinical approach to dealing with bereavement issues. May be a good reference preparing for a presentation.

Loss & Grief in Medicine, Bailliere Tindall; 1978. Deals with various types of loss related to medical conditions or genetics, including surgeries, infertility and many other situations.

Helping Bereaved Children: A Handbook for Practitioners, Nancy Boyd Webb 1993. Provides different techniques to use with children to help them deal with the death of a loved one, including parent, grandparent, sibling, other relatives or friends.

Healing the Bereaved Child , Alan Wolfelt; 1996. This book balances the role of grief counselor and provides helpful hints for working with children who are grieving. The book includes a great bibliography with age appropriate books.

Biopsychosocial Aspects of Bereavement, Sidney Zisook, 1987. Professional assessment book geared towards those who are dealing with a group of students to help them gather pertinent information.

Books about Sudden Death & Suicide

Living With Grief After Sudden Loss - Kenneth Doka; 1996 - This book presents a series of short situations in which a death occurred including suicide, disasters, heart attack, etc. Good book to refer in order to understand more of the dynamics of sudden death.

Suicide Survivors' Handbook, Trudy Carlson, 1995. A guide for the bereaved and those who wish to help them. Written by a mother whose 14 year old son committed suicide

Suicide: Prevention, Intervention and Postvention, Earl Grollman; 1971. This book addresses the issues of suicide and is written for professionals who are working with the survivors or their family members.

Making Sense of Suicide: An in-depth look at why people kill themselves , David Lester, 1997. Based on modern research, this book examines suicide and the reasons someone may choose to take their own life. This book may be helpful to professionals more than survivors.

A Message of Hope for Surviving the Tragedy of Suicide, Patricia Harness-Overley, 1992. Written by a woman whose 18 year old son committed suicide. She takes a year long approach to help others deal with the feelings and emotions related to a death by suicide. Good for use by survivors of suicide.

Catalogs

Abbey Press
St. Meinrad, IN 47577
1-800-325-2511
abbeypress.com
carenotes.com

A Place to Remember
1885 University Avenue W, #110
St. Paul, MN 55104
1-800-631-0973
aplacetoremember.com

Batesville Management Services
One Batesville Boulevard
Batesville, IN 47006
1-800-622-8373 ext. 7788
batesville.com

Centering Corporation
P.O. Box 4600
Omaha, NE 68104
402-553-1200
centering.org

Compassion Books
7036 Highway 80 South
Burnsville, NC 28714
1-800-970-4220
compassionbooks.com

In-Sight Books
P.O. Box 42467
Oklahoma City, OK 73123
insightbooks.com

Living With Loss
Bereavement Publishing
P.O. Box 61
1-888-604-4673
Montrose, CO 81402
livingwithloss.com

Ohio Funeral Director's Association
2501 North Star Rd.
P.O. Box 21760
Columbus, OH 43221
ohio-fda.org

Willowgreen
10351 Dawson's Creek Blvd. #B
Ft. Wayne, IN 46825
willowgreen.com

Note Regarding Video Use

It is particularly important to review videos prior to use with a client or patient. Some are educational, while others are supportive. Some deal specifically with cancer while others are for those who are facing and accepting the fact that they are actively dying.

Videos of General Interest

A Ray of Hope - Facing the Holidays Following A Loss People who have loss a spouse, fiancée, parent or other loved one discuss ways they prepared for significant holidays following the death of a loved one. Narrated by Paul Alexander who discusses ways people can adjust and prepare for "holidays." Good for general use. (38 minutes) 1997

Before I Die: Medical Care & Personal Choices (1997). A panel of specialist discuss decisions that patients and family members face when a chronic or terminal illness is diagnosed. The video is a PBS special that addresses emotional as well as practical issues related to end-of-life decisions. Useful for training sessions, group presentations and for some patients/family members. (60 minutes)

Common Threads-Stories from the Quilt (1989). Tells the story of five individuals who died or are dying from AIDS. The "story tellers" include a wife, partner, parents, significant other and a patient. Relays the pain of death related to this disease. Some of the facts are dated but the information and emotions are relevant for today. A good teaching tape about AIDS and the emotions related to the diagnosis and death. (79 minutes)

DEATH: The Trip of a Lifetime. 4 tape series that addresses various aspects of death & dying. First video, The Chasm, explores death and dying from 12 different countries/cultures. It also highlights an elementary school that teaches a course on death & dying.

Second video, The Good Death, explores how people view a "good death", including various cultures. Third video, Letting Go, explores funerals and the rituals associated with funerals in various cultures. Fourth Video, Going for Glory, explores how different cultures manifest belief in "afterlife" and how their belief may affect their life in this world. The videos would be helpful for training staff about culturally diverse views on death. (Each video is 60 minutes) 1993

Ethical Issues: Who Lives? Who Dies? Dateline. (1997) - A Dateline interview which deals with several ethical situations related to end of life issues. Video is good for group presentations, ethical presentations, or for teaching purposes. (50 minutes)

Harbor of Hope. This video interviews people who are dealing with chronic illnesses such as cancer, MS, AIDS, etc. The video emphasizes the power of hope and a positive attitude when dealing with a chronic illness. (37 minutes) 1994

Invincible Summer-Returning to Life after You're Loved One Has Died - Narrated video that integrates nature, music & words to discuss the pain of loss. The stages of grief are shared as is the fact that grief is universal. Good for mediation or for use with a client in between visits. General loss is discussed and can be used with mixed bereavement groups. Appropriate for those who lost a loved one in the past year. (16 minutes) 1989

It's In Every One of Us (1987). Meditative video based on the song of the same name, features faces of people who display loss, despair, hope, laughter and happiness. Good for use with groups as a way to start conversation or to conclude a presentation on a hopeful side. Appropriate for all ages. (5 minutes)

Living With Grief: Children Mourning, Mourning Children - Panel discussion sponsored by the National Hospice Organization. Discusses children & grief and how parents, educators and other professionals can help children deal with grief. (60 minutes) 1993

The Pitch of Grief (1985). Several adults discuss their loss, including how they were told of the death and how they dealt with their feelings. Good for use with clients, groups or professionals. (27 minutes)

Rainbow's Remedy (1992). Parts of this video will be good to use with children or teens while other parts would be good for adults. It would also be good to use if you are doing a presentation for those who will be facilitating bereavement support groups. Preview prior to use. (22 minutes)

Shadowlands - A film about C.S. Lewis when his wife died from cancer. A moving film about the struggles faced when a couple deals with cancer. (73 minutes) 1985

To Touch A Grieving Heart. Good video to use with professionals or those who facilitate bereavement support groups. Addresses issues of death from several perspectives and provides insight to what the bereaved feel. (40 minutes) 1995

We Will Remember: A meditation for those who live on - A short meditative video that uses nature scenery to discuss memories and the fact the "memories" will always be a part of the life of someone who lost a loved one. (10 minutes) 1992

Whose Death Is It Anyway? - A look at the human side of end-of-life decision making in an emotionally charged PBS special. Includes professionals & family members. (1 hr) 1996

Whitewater: The Positive Power of Grief. Utilizes nature to discuss the experience of death and loss. The film is narrated and does not provide a "discussion" format. Good for use with an individual client or with a support group. Best use is with those who lose someone in the past year. (12 minutes) 1991

Videos about Anticipatory Grief

Living Fully Until Death. This tape interviews two dying patients, one of cancer and one of ALS. The film follows these two people for two years and the effect on them and their families as they face their illness and the choices they must make. A good video for patients and their families. (28 minutes) 1996

ABC News Special: Lessons in Living with Morrie Schwartz - Ted Koepel interview Morrie Schwartz over a six month period as he prepares for the progression of his ALS disease and his death. Inspirational video.   (1 hour) 1996

Dateline Special: Preparing for Death. Interviews a woman who prepared for her death by video taping stories for her daughter. She prepared tapes to be viewed by her daughter when she was older. Her daughter is 3. The young woman is about 35 and died of breast cancer. (30 minutes) 1998

Videos for Adults

The Courage to Grieve - A creative living, recovery and growth through grief video by Judy Tautelbaum. The video is based on her book and would be useful for support groups, presentations and professional training. (45minutes) 1994

Men and Grief. Eight men who have experienced grief in their lives discuss what it feels like to be a man and to grieve. The loses include wives, children, parents, & siblings. The group is diverse in age and ethnic background. Deaths were sudden as well as anticipated. Appropriate for groups, individuals and for training sessions. (60 minutes) 1995

Grown Up Tears: Adults Grieving the Death of a Parent - This video interviews 6 adults who lost one of their parents from a variety of illnesses or sudden death. It addresses their relationship with the deceased parent and how they have felt since the death. Deaths occurred from 3 weeks to 4 years. Does not address the stages of grieving. (28 minutes) 1994

Videos about Cancer Grief

Castles in the Sand: Facing Leukemia. Josh Littman, a newscaster who was diagnosed with leukemia in 1986 utilized his journalistic skills to capture the process of dealing with his diagnosis. His journey is captured on film, through the experience of his family, the medical team and his friends. Josh died from leukemia a year after his diagnosis. The film deals realistically with the disease and the effect it has on the patient, the family and those who are involved with the care of the patient. Not recommended for patients diagnosed with leukemia but might be helpful for follow up bereavement for surviving family members or for use with staff training. (60 minutes) 1995

Three Days Out: Four Women, One Struggle. This two set series discusses the struggles that four women faced as breast cancer patients. They are part of a breast cancer support group who partakes in a "ropes course, outward bound" type of experience. The videos interview four women who discuss the challenges they faced with their diagnosis and treatment. (Video 1-34 minutes; Video 2-22 minutes) 1997

ABC News Special: The Race for a Cure. Provides an update on the latest treatments and drugs that are being developed as well as interviews with patients and survivors. Good tape for educational presentations and use with some clients. (45 minutes) 1998

Handle with Care: Living with Metastatic Cancer (1998) Dramatization of how it feels to deal with Metastatic cancer. Very well done, captures multitude of feelings. (26 min.)

Unwanted Challenges: Facing a Cancer Diagnosis - This video interviews seven individuals whose lives have been affected by cancer. Five have cancer and two are family members. This video would be useful for newly diagnosed individuals and their families in order to help them deal with their emotions and discuss the effect it could have on their families. (25 minutes) 1996

Videos for Children & Adolescents

Children Grieve, Too (1996). A good tape for use with teachers, counselors, parents or a general audience in order to help them understand how to talk with children about death and how to allow children to mourn. Culturally diverse. (30 min.)

A Child's Grief. This video interviews several children as part of a support group. They discuss their feelings and reactions to the death of their siblings or parents. The video also interviews a few parents about the death and how they perceive the situation. This tape would be helpful for teachers, parents and other professionals who work with children. Parts of the tape would be helpful for children to view. Age appropriate for elementary to middle school age children. (45 minutes) 1994

A Child's View of Grief. Narrated by Alan Wolfelt, children teach adults about allowing children to grief. Good for use with parents, educators or professionals. Also good for use with children in order to get them to talk about their feelings. (25 minutes) 1996

The Fall of Freddie the Leaf. Culturally diverse film that addresses the issues of life and death, from the view of the changing seasons. Appropriate for school age children through adults. (17 minutes) 1985

Standing Tall: A video about teen grief (1994). This tape interviews six teens who have lost a loved one including a grandfather, brother, father, aunt and cousin. Types of deaths include natural death, cancer, suicide and homicide. The tape could be helpful in starting conversations about death and dying. (20 minutes)

What About Me? Kids and Grief. This is an excellent video for use with children and those who work with children. The video interviews a group of multi-cultural children about their grief. The kids talk about the effect an illness has on the family or how the death affected the family. This is a powerful video for pre-school to junior high children. (18 minutes) 1993

The Tomorrows Children Face When A Parent Dies - This video interviews children,elementary to collage age, who lost a parent due to illness or sudden death. This is an excellent video for professionals who work with children as well as for use with children

Videos for Widows & Widowers

The Longest Journey. Widows/widowers describe their personal journey after the death of their spouse. The video includes widows and widowers, young and old, culturally diverse. Integrates some "docudrama" to highlight feelings, emotions, etc. Professionals address issues of grief and loss throughout the video. Discusses new relationships and remarriage. The effect of the death on other family members is briefly discussed. (53 minutes) 1992

You're Not Alone: Coping with the Death of a Spouse. This video interviews five people who have lost a spouse. Some of the deaths were expected while others were not. This is not a culturally diverse tape. Would be good to use with a support group. (40 minutes) 1995

Websites

i-remember.org a site designed to allow people to share journal entries in a safe and supportive environment. (Centering Corporation)

fireinmyheart.com a site designed for bereaved teens to share stories, illustrations, journal entries and other information in an on-line anonymous environment. (Centering Corporation)

counselingstlouis.net Sibling Loss resources. The website is overseen by a bereaved sibling and offers readings and other resources.

ncptsd.org National Center for Post Traumatic Stress Disorder

dougy.org National center for grieving children. They offer a lot of resources and materials for families.

About the Author

Biographical Sketch

Rev. Daniel M. Newman, PhD, DD
Holistic Health Consultant
and Senior Health Educator

Rev. Dr. Daniel M. Newman is an interfaith minister who holds both Doctor of Philosophy and Doctor of Divinity degrees from the American Institute of Holistic Theology. Dan is certified as an HIV/AIDS Prevention Specialist (APS), Risk Reduction Specialist (RRS), and as a Senior Health Educator. He was a group facilitator for New Dads sponsored by the National Fatherhood Initiative. Dan was Certified in Thanatology by the Association for Death Education and Counseling.

In 1995 he was ordained by the state of Ohio and in 2002 became sole proprietor of a Holistic Health Consulting business. Rev. Newman has many years' experience working with people in recovery, the incarcerated, and people on death row, which is why he decided to write this book.

Dan takes great pride as an artist, author, humorist, and national keynote plenary speaker, and workshop provider.

Honors & Awards

Certificate of Appreciation in recognition of valuable contributions and the many years of service to the members of the Kentucky Association of EMTs and to the KAEMT Spring Fling conference 2009.

American Red Cross for participation in the Gulf Coast Mass Care Sheltering Project for Hurricane Season 2006.

American Red Cross recognition for valuable service during the 2005 hurricane season relief efforts.

Katrina Relief "05" Certificate of Appreciation for valuable service during the Hurricane Katrina relief effort.

State of Ohio Department of Health certification of completion of Client Centered Counseling.

EMS Week Award Presented to Dan Newman for Years of Dedicated Involvement in EMS Education.

Urban League of Greater Cincinnati Honors Rev. Dan Newman for dedication to HIV/AIDS Awareness in the African American Community.

Certificate of Appreciation and Achievement in Continuous HIV/AIDS Education Prevention for the Deaf Communities of Greater Cincinnati and Northern Kentucky.

Covington Police Citizen Academy completion award.

Hospice of Northern Kentucky Certificate of Appreciation for Outstanding Community and Volunteer HIV/AIDS Educational Programs.

Jefferson Alcohol & Drug Abuse Center Certificate of Recognition for Continuous HIV Education in the Substance Abusing Community.

State of Ohio Authority to Solemnize Marriages having produced credentials of his being a Regularly Ordained and Licensed Minister in Bereavement and After Care Services.

Morehead State University Health, Physical Education and Recreation Certificate 0f Appreciation for presenting at the KAHPERD Summer Workshop Meeting the KERA Challenge!

Certificate of Achievement Award by the Administrative Office of the Courts and the Division of Juvenile Services in HIV/AIDS Prevention and Education.

Image In-Sights, Inc. Letter of Thanks for Continuous Education Unit Nurses Training and Certification in HIV/AIDS Education and Prevention Transmission.

ETHICON ENDO-SURGERY, Inc of Johnson & Johnson Company Certificate of Appreciation for Outstanding Work in the Field of HIV/AIDS Education and Prevention.

Housing Authority of Covington Fitness & Career Center Letter of Extreme Gratitude.

The Kentucky AIDS Training and Education Center, a partner of the Great Lakes/Tennessee Valley AIDS Education and Training Center. Department of Preventive Medicine and Environmental

Health University of Kentucky Medical Center. To certify the Dan Newman has successfully completed KATEC Trainer HIV Workshop KY CHR Series #: 1297-876-M.

Eastern Kentucky University Division of Substance Abuse in recognition of successful completion of "Preventing HIV Disease among Substance Abusers - Training of the Trainers" in conjunction with continuing Education Units CHR Series #0812-621M.

National Institute on Drug Abuse Community Education on Research and Practice Project CERTIFICATE OF COMPLETION for

Participation in the Prevention Communication for Diverse Populations, Miami, Florida.

Northern Kentucky Health Department VOLUNTEER RECOGNITION WEEK to congratulate and THANK YOU for your contributions and diligence in promoting a healthier community for Northern Kentucky.

Talbert House Certification of Appreciation In Recognition of Participation in "Men in Recovery Month" Extended Treatment Program.

Certifications

Multi-disciplinarian HIV/AIDS Education Curriculum approved by the Cabinet for Human Services as required by KY CHR Series.

Ministry ordination given by the State of Ohio, Authority to Solemnize Marriages.

Center for Disease Control and Prevention (CDC) Ask, Screen, Intervene, (ASI) Module 1-4, EV1325

Kentucky Board of EMS Training and Educational Institution 03/31/2013

Cincinnati STD/HIV Mid-West Prevention Training Center Faculty Member & North/Eastern Regional Prevention Specialist

Women's Crisis Center of Northern KY Volunteer for victims of male rape

State of Ohio Department of Health Client Centered Counseling ODH Testing and Counseling #3179

CSAT Grant Program Advisory Board Member of Thunder Child Inner Tribal Treatment Center,Sheridan WY.

Dan Newman, PhD, DD

Connect with the author:

Dan Newman
4015 Cherry Street, Suite #34
Cincinnati, OH 45223

Email – dan@GriefBehindBars.com

www.ingramcontent.com/pod-product-compliance
Lightning Source LLC
LaVergne TN
LVHW091215080426
835509LV00009B/1008